T0208475

The Age of *Wonderful* NONSENSE

Finding P.E.A.C.E
and Navigating Your 20's

RYAN W. JONES

Edited By
Kristy M. Hunter
Bailey Steinhauser

BALBOA.
PRESS
A DIVISION OF HAY HOUSE

Balboa Press books may be ordered through booksellers or by contacting:

Balboa Press
A Division of Hay House
1663 Liberty Drive
Bloomington, IN 47403
www.balboapress.com
1 (877) 407-4847

Print information available on the last page.

ISBN: 978-1-9822-0893-6 (sc)
ISBN: 978-1-9822-0895-0 (hc)
ISBN: 978-1-9822-0894-3 (e)

Library of Congress Control Number: 2018908499

Balboa Press rev. date: 07/26/2018

ENDORSEMENTS
Words From Actual Humans

"A modern sifting and weaving of the wisdom of self-help, 12 Step, and spiritual traditions into a unique roadmap for change...by and for Millenials... and us all. A must-read for high school seniors, their parents, and all college students...a vivid account of how to get lost and find yourself again." - Jerry Duprez PhD., Author of *"A Sack Half Full"*

"Ryan has a unique ability to discuss serious, deep-seated issues while also allowing readers to be entertained with his humorous, yet insightful, personal journey. Navigating your 20s is not an easy feat, but Ryan gives hope to the hopeless with a road-map to fighting the daily battles of life." Ethan Chapman, Christ Follower, Former Professional Baseball Player and Amateur Advisor at Full Circle Sports Management

"The Age of Wonderful Nonsense is a brutally honest, humorous take on the road to recovery. Not just for twenty-something, but instead, for anyone who needs inspiration as they need to make changes in their lives and are looking for tools that they can continue to utilize time and time again. You will laugh, cry, reflect, build, and above all, be inspired to change your habits, and ultimately, your life." -Kristy M. Hunter, Copy Editor and High School English Teacher

The Age of Wonderful Nonsense is honest, refreshing and can help anyone find their own unequivocal happiness in a healthy, lasting way. An impressive balance of humor and raw honesty that will have any reader ready to take that first step towards a more sustained life." Bailey Steinhauser, Public Relations and Copy Editor

"The Age of Wonderful Nonsense reminds us that every living thing on this planet goes through periods of growth, in one way or another. Some of us grow physically, some grow mentally, and others grow emotionally - all at different stages in our lives. Everything that happens to us eventually intertwines and comes full circle. But, remembering that our biological clock will always be different from anothers' is central to our growth as humans. This book reminds me that happiness and success will always be found by those who come searching, as well as work hard for it!" Braun Wilburn, Fitness Model and Health Coach

To My Loving Family –
Dad, Mom, Austin and Jessica…

May the hope and compassion you
instilled in me live on through the peace
I intend to bring this broken world.

CONTENTS

AUTHOR'S NOTE

Dear Parents,

I guess it's only fair that I begin by addressing the people who can truly make all the difference in shaping young minds. Yes, you, parents, have all the power – and as we know, with great power comes great... head-ache. Lucky you.

I'm sure you're all very worried for your child to find their place in this world. As you should be – after all, you created them. But, I'd like to point out a few things first. Amongst the kids who will be sitting in classrooms around the world there is an author, who probably cares little about Geometry... There is a musician and artist who aren't interested in English or Government. There is an athlete whose natural ability is far more important than learning about Bill Nye in science class...And there is an entrepreneur who probably hates the classroom all together.

If your child is a high achiever, then terrific — nicely done, we're all very proud of you. But, if he or she struggles in some areas…please do not degrade and deny them the freedom to define their own identity and American Dream. Tell them it's okay. Say that you believe in their dreams and would like to be a part of them. Explain to them that some people take longer than others to find their passion, but that you support them in whatever they want to do with their lives.

Once you do this, sit back in your comfy recliner and watch your child take over the world. Doctors, lawyers and business management consultants are not the only people who are happy in this life. Your child will be happy too…if you allow them to be.

You can begin by giving them this book on how to get lost, and find yourself again :)

Enjoy, friends.

#Lost20Something

PROLOGUE

"Ryan,

You are such a gift; such a treasure. Your expansive heart and compassionate ways are so admirable. You have so many gifts — like being able to connect with just about anyone, having a wonderful sense of humor, and loving people despite their differences. We both have such a drive in us to want to make an impact in this world. We both crave a change in society, and we both know that we can be that change.

I feel like you're growing and going to grow more this year. I know different circumstances can carry a ton of weight, but I also know that you're Ryan — you can do anything you set your heart to.

On my birthday this year, we drove home together and had a conversation that still plays on my heart. We talked about relationships and what we look for in others. There is so much value in that, and as you take this journey I want you to know that I pray often for your future and for your "now". I pray you stay true to your character and put value in things of real worth.

People change, and plans change, but family is constant and forever. You have taught me that. So, I write this to you to let you know that I look up to you, and I'm proud to say you're my brother. I see you making a difference in this world already. Do not let others dwindle your spirit, love, and compassion.

As you take this journey of life, your heart undertakes many intense things. We both love to write – even if no one will ever read it besides us. So, this journal is just for that purpose alone. Write your pain, your plans, your thoughts, and your actions. Write a list of people you want to help, and how you can do that. Write down what you want in your future wife, and what you don't – and maybe one day you can give her that page. Write your standards and your dreams. Through this, you can physically see your heart on paper. Make it a daily habit, and something you hold value to. Write letters to people – even if you never give it to them. Write letters to yourself, and write letters to God. Put your anger, love, joy, irritation, dreams into words, and one day you can look back and see your journey. Sometimes it's not about the destination, but about the journey you take to get *there. This journal can be your "Journey Journal." It can be whatever you want.*

I love you so much Ryan, and seeing your heart has been such a privilege. My whole life you've always been someone I see as inspirational. What I love most about you is that whatever you seek, your heart is there too. Keep being you, because lives are already being impacted by you…mine included, no doubt.

Happy Birthday, Brother.

May this year be a defining season of your life. We'll change the world, starting today & forever. I love you more than words.

-Sissy
Be the Change. Be the Difference. Go the distance. Take the Journey."
May 31, 2016

I found that letter while standing on the edge of my window deciding if it was worth it to even be alive anymore. It was a time when I had nothing in my life to hope for and only myself to blame for it.

My sister, Jessica (or as I like to call her, *Blessica)*, is the most selfless, empathetic person I know. She wrote that letter and gave me my Journey Journal on my 26th birthday without having a clue in the world that I was lost in the darkest place I had ever been. She was only seventeen at the time and little did she know, she would be my inspiration for changing my life and writing this book.

She prayed every day for two years that I would find peace and happiness again. Even though she is my younger sister, I admire and look to her for guidance in all areas of my life. She is remarkable, in every way a person can be, and she saved me from the lowest point I have ever been.

She understands the true meaning of life…to love and cherish every person we share the journey with. I love her more than words can describe, and she deserves the credit for saving my life and helping me find my peace. I owe it to her to help as many people as I can do the same.

My great hope is that our mission on this quest of life will not be to simply survive but to come alive through passion, purpose and ultimately peace. I believe that we become what we are committed to.

I may have a background in pain, but I am committed to a future in P.E.A.C.E.

This is my Peace Quest.

INTRODUCTION

So, What is the Age of Wonderful Nonsense?

Well, have you heard my joke about the Roaring 20's? Never mind, the ending is too depressing...see what I did there? Before we dive into navigating your own roaring 20's, let's take a BRIEF (I know how you millennials are) history lesson into a decade filled with glamour, endless possibilities, and rapid growth.

The 1920's, or the Age of Wonderful Nonsense (as I like to call it), was not only a decade of dramatic social and cultural change – it was one roaring time to be alive. For the first time in American history, people decided to ditch the farm and live the thriving city life. New and exciting fads took the world by storm. Wealth in the nation doubled, flappers raced to fill new jazz clubs, skirts rose above the knee, and The American Dream was alive and well.

One of the strangest fads of the Roaring Twenties, in which perfectly describes why I refer to this era as the Age of Wonderful Nonsense, was flagpole sitting. Yes, you read that right. Alvin "Shipwreck" Kelly, who was born in Hell's Kitchen in 1893, became famous in the 1920's for flagpole sitting - making as much as $1000 a week. Who knew that sitting on your butt doing absolutely nothing could result in $1000 a week? What a time to be alive.

In 1924, Alvin's first 'sitting' took place in Los Angeles in which he posted for an impressive thirteen hours and thirteen minutes. He would later sit on a pole for 12 days straight - shattering his previous record of 7. Flagpole sitting became a national phenomenon with people everywhere chomping at the bit to be the next, "King of the Pole" (sorry strippers of today, you were not the first masters of the pole).

Hard to believe that a guy who lost his mother at childbirth, father shortly after, would then go from sailor and failed boxer to world-famous stunt performer. Alvin, who referred to himself as the "Luckiest Fool on Earth," claimed to have survived five shipwrecks (including Titanic), three car crashes, two airplane crashes, one train wreck – and a partridge in a pear tree. I think we can all agree that Alvin is one wonderfully fascinating human.

Though Alvin was able to survive countless years of

poleing (I think that's what the kids call it) and numerous crashes, there was one crash he was unable to survive – the stock market crash in October of 1929. Flagpole sitting, among many other exciting new fads, slowly faded away with the dawn of The Great Depression. As Alvin tragically put it, "the stock market crash had killed pole-sitting...people couldn't stand anything higher than their busted securities." It was a sad day for Alvin, along with many other American Dreams in the Roaring 20's.

Alright Dude, Why Do I Care?

So, why on earth am I sitting here (pun intended) talking about some weirdo who sat on a flagpole in the 1920's? I'm glad you asked. The Roaring 20's, and Alvin, can teach us a lot about navigating our own Age of Wonderful Nonsense. Though we may be unaware, our twenties are a defining decade of our lives. It's a season of transition filled with endless possibilities, forward momentum, self-discovery, and if you're not careful – a Great Depression.

Before we get too carried away, let's recap. Life before your twenties was relatively straight forward. You went to school, kept your dog from eating your homework, played a few sports, tried not to kill your parents, and inevitably got your diploma. Then, the options are, go to college, join the military, attend a trade school, or find a job. You meet tons of people, learn new perspectives, hit a beer bong or two (sorry mom), and laugh your face off with all your new friends.

Then, out of nowhere, the storms start swirling in. Your car breaks down on the way to the job you absolutely hate. The laundry is piling up, in front of the door, in the one-bedroom apartment you can barely afford. The girlfriend (or boyfriend) you invested all your time into turns out to be a total psychopath. You become that old weirdo still going to the same clubs and bars you went to when you thought you were cool. You watch Netflix all day, Sunday, trying to avoid the anxiety of Monday morning. You pound coffee in the breakroom dreading the voice of chipper old Jan who sits in the cubicle next to you. The only exciting part of your life is Friday, at 5pm, when you sprint out of your office calling every human in your contacts for happy hour. Sound vaguely familiar?

We're all the same, in one way or another. We buy the same goods, listen to the same music, get the same cubicle jobs, binge watch the same *Stranger Things,* and seek the same approval from our peers. It doesn't matter how different you think you are, we're all trying to do the same things and solve the same problems. We all want to belong. We all feel the urge to connect.

For centuries, humans have always searched for a sense of belonging, an identity to call our own. This longing for purpose exists in all of us and serves as our compass for navigating through life. I believe we, as humans, are always curiously inclined to push the limits and see what else we can do. We have a knack for always wanting more, even if it means forgetting who we once were.

It's interesting how one decision, good or bad, can alter the direction of your life for years to come. One minute, you're surrounded by countless friends in a thriving world filled with new fads and endless opportunity. You're ambitious and hopeful the future will always be this exciting. You push off your problems because, hey, that's what everyone else is doing and look at them – they're happy. Or so it seems.

The next minute, your need of approval rips apart your American dream of doing something remarkable with your life. You allow outside influences to force you into being someone you're not. You lie to yourself and claim you are doing the right things to better your life. You lose yourself completely, and the saddest part is you don't even realize it at the time.

At least that's how it was for me. To be fair though, I'm not the only one who didn't have it all figured out. No one actually knows what the hell they're doing in their roaring twenties. There's too much pressure on us to have it all figured out. The moment we slip up or don't know exactly what the next move is, we're made to feel like we're worthless and incapable of achieving our dreams.

Society has this image of who we're supposed to be and what our lives should look like. So, what do we do? We slap on a fake smile, snap the picture, mock it up with a few pretty filters, post it on social media, and wait for the dopamine hits with every new like. Sounds like a recipe for another Great Depression if you ask me.

But don't worry, it's only as depressing as you make it. There is a flagpole out there waiting for all of us to climb up and pop a squat on. Though my Roaring Twenties resulted in a similar Great Depression, I finally decided to take control of my life and create my own American Dream.

And so will you, we've only just begun.

WEATHERING THE SH*T STORM

(Sorry for the language, Mom, but it's a title so we're good, right?)

"Most great people have attained their greatest success just one step beyond their greatest failure."

—Napoleon Hill

Have you ever heard of Saturn's Return? I know, me neither. I sure wish I knew what it was a few years earlier, though. It might have made things a heck of a lot easier.

Though most of us have never heard of it, I guarantee you have either been through it, are about to get blasted with it, or you are currently buried alive in the trenches of the infamous Saturn's Return.

Okay Guy, What Is It?

In short, it's the astrological term for "Quarter Life Crisis." It's the period in your life when the universe decides it's your turn to go through the ringer.

Basically, every 27 to 29 years, Saturn completes its orbit around the sun and returns to the same zodiac sign it was in when you graced us with your presence at birth.

Your first Saturn Return, which usually happens between the ages of 26 and 30 (but not always), is a defining season of your life. It's a metaphorical rebirth advancing you into a new stage of adulthood.

This period of your life is brutal. I won't sit here and sugar coat it. It will break you, shake you, and flip your entire universe upside down. You will come face to face with demons you didn't know existed and be forced to look them dead in the eye.

I know this because I experienced my own Saturn's Return and lived to talk about it…barely. Ryan 1, Saturn 0.

I'll never forget the day when my rock bottom came and my entire universe crumbled around me. It was on that day when I was at my lowest of lows and had absolutely nothing in my life except for a mountain of problems. That was the day I decided to change my life. That was the day I decided it was time to move on and be the person I always dreamed of becoming. It was time for me stop depending on everyone else for my happiness and finally stand on my own two feet.

That was the day I began my Peace Quest.

Life In Your 20's

Being in your 20's is like losing your parents at Disneyland, but for the rest of your life. Sure, it's all fun and games because at least Mickey Mouse is there, and cotton candy is flowing. Then you realize, "Wait, what the heck am I supposed to do now? MOM, DAAAAAD!?!"

It's almost like we're the lost generation. We're told what to do our entire lives, by people who are probably just as lost as we are, and then we're expected to take what we are told and somehow apply it to a life we never truly wanted. Then, when we ask questions, we're made to feel even more lost and told we're never going to amount to anything. And then, we get pounded with failure after failure and are expected to roll with the punches. Until, one day, we've run for so fast and so long that we can barely stand on our own two feet anymore. Then, we're forgotten about. Pushed to the side and told to wait it out, the storm will one day clear.

Does that sound about right, or is it just me?

Life, relatively speaking, is one giant sh*t storm. And the worst part is, there isn't a weatherman standing by to tell us the storm is coming. Adulting is like looking both ways before you cross the street and then getting hit by a hurricane. The only difference is these hurricanes sweep through our lives in the forms of people, decisions, social acceptance, depression, and failure. They hit us over and over, forcing us down a path of self-destruction. This is why being an adult, sucks – royally.

Do you remember how giddy we used to be on Christmas morning when we walked down the stairs and the little red bike was there waiting for us? Or when we found the $5 under our pillow after we lost our first tooth? Or how amazing it felt when we scored our first goal, got our first 'A,' had our first crush? Yeah, me either. Let's be real -these small, yet profound joys, slowly evaporate with time.

Children can teach us many things about how we should view the world as adults. From my childhood, I learned how to embrace new life experiences and be confident in myself. I was always very motivated to be the best I could be at everything. I learned how to be curious, happy for what I do have, and fight for what I want in life. I was at peace with my surroundings and upbringing, so it was easy to be happy (thanks Mom and Dad for not leaving me lost at Disneyland).

A child's imagination is a beautiful thing if you can figure out what the hell they're talking about. Children usually have a very positive outlook on the way the world works. As a child, I was no different. I was the giddiest human on the planet as I laid in bed the night before Christmas. I tied my tooth to every door knob I could find to get that next $5. I would even steal the ball from my own teammate if I had to, just to get that exciting feeling of scoring again. It wasn't until I experienced real pain in my life when my understanding of the way the world works began to shift.

I think over time, our souls harden. Different friend groups move on, girlfriends and boyfriends become exes. We're hit with past failures, mean people, and dead end jobs over and over again. Soon enough, we become shut off. Having an imagination and hope for a better tomorrow becomes something we used to know, but soon forgot.

Some people are lucky. They know exactly what they want out of life early on and are relentless in attaining it. Good for them – they deserve it. Most of us, however, are forced to continuously alter our path, always striving to reinvent ourselves and find our passion somewhere along the way. Whichever category you fall in, at one point or another, we all find ourselves lost, trying to navigate our way through the storm. Basically, we're all just roaming around aimlessly, hoping we don't get swooped up by a hurricane when we cross the street on the way to work today.

Whatever walk (or storm) you're on, there's no doubt in my mind that you seek more out of this life. Whether you are a successful businessperson, aspiring actor, camp counselor, Olympic ice sculptor, educator, parent, cage fighter, or lost soul (like I was) – we all have an inner longing to unlock our greatest potential and live the life we've always wanted. Regardless of how well you're doing or not, deep inside all of us resides a passion limitless beyond what we believe to be capable of.

Life is a series of choices. Every new day carries with it a string of unanswered questions and decisions to be made that will positively or negatively affect our future. Over time, we become consumed with "should haves" from the past and "should I's" for the future. 'I should have chosen a different career path…maybe then I'd be more successful. I should have never dated her/him… If I didn't, I wouldn't feel so lost now. Maybe I should have drank less in college and applied myself. Should I get out of bed today, or roll over and enjoy the little comfort I do have? Should I try to find my passion, or just continue going through the motions and surviving?

We become consumed with *'shoulding'* all over ourselves. Yes, you read that right. *'Shoulding'* all over yourself is the act of living entirely in the past, beating yourself up for wrong turns you've made along the way. This act only harms our ability to grow into the person we want to be. We all have pasts we are not proud of but it's what we do with our 'now' that will define our future.

You're Not The Only One...

What if I told you that you're not the only one fighting a battle today? What if I went even further to tell you that behind every successful person there are many unsuccessful years filled with struggle, failure, and the same 'should haves' that we're fighting today? Would you believe me? Or would you think I was just "that guy" trying to be inspiring and tell you there is light at the end of the tunnel? Well, why don't we let you be the judge?

Once upon a time, there was a young girl born into poverty in rural Mississippi to a 13-year-old single mother. That young girl was later molested during her childhood and became pregnant at 14, only to lose her child in infancy. After surviving a tough childhood, she packed bags in a grocery store to put herself through college. Then, in her 20's, she was fired from her job hosting the 6 p.m. news slot at Baltimore's WJZ-TV in 1977. She went on record to say, "I had no idea what I was in for or that this was going to be the greatest growing period of my adult life" (*Baltimore Sun*). Fast-forward to now - that same 'girl' is known as, "The Queen of Daytime Television" while being one of the greatest philanthropists in American History and labeled as the most influential woman in the world. Yes, her name is Oprah Winfrey.

Meanwhile, over in Dallas, there was a 25-year-old bartender who had just graduated from Indiana University and was trying to find his place in the world. He found himself, "sleeping on the floor with six guys in a three-bedroom apartment," (*How To Win at the Sport of Business*). After moving on from his dead-end bartending job, he took a sales job at a PC software retailer. He was soon fired after meeting with a client trying to close a deal instead of opening the store. He later revealed that he used to drive around looking at big houses, imagining what it would be like to live in them and used that as his motivation. Fast-forward to now – that struggling bartender has a net worth of over $3 Billion and spends his nights watching the Dallas Mavericks from the owner's box. Yes, indeed, he is our favorite Shark, Mark Cuban.

Oh, and how can we forget our beloved 25-year-old secretary, over in London, who came up with her claim to fame while on a 4-hour delayed train in 1990. Though her imagination was one in a million, it would take her countless years of struggle, depression, and failure before delivering that mind to the world. In that period, she saw the death of her mother, birth of her first child, divorce from her first husband and poverty. She went from living on welfare to being a multi-millionaire within five years. Thank you, J.K. Rowling, for believing in yourself enough to give us, *Harry Potter*.

Still not convinced? Alright, well, have you done any online shopping lately? I bet you didn't know that it was a McDonald's 'grill man' by the name of Jeff Bezos who would go on to be the Founder of Amazon and worth around $90 Billion today. Oh, and did you happen to do that shopping on a Mac? Whether you love him or hate him, you should, without a doubt, respect the genius of Steve Jobs who altered the course of mainstream computing. He went from being put up for adoption, at birth, and later dropping out of college, to pioneering the microcomputer and having a net worth exceeding $10

Billion. Jobs taught us that, "the people who are crazy enough to think they can change the world are the ones who do."

So, what do these remarkable humans have in common? *Perseverance*…or, as I like to call it, *Weathering the Sh*t Storm*. They believed in themselves enough to overcome adversity and persevere into living a successful, peaceful, and purpose-filled life.

This world is full of sh*t storms. I believe we, at one point or another, walk directly into the storm of our lives and we are certainly not prepared for it. Clouds settle in and the next steps are uncertain. The road has narrowed, and the vision becomes foggy and unclear.

When we're young, the vision is clear and anything is possible. We believe in our dreams and embrace the future. We're happy (usually), full of life, and ambitious to conquer the world. As time passes, self-doubt creeps in, and the negative force of the world tilts us from pursuing our dreams. Soon enough, we are forced to abide by the rules society has laid out for us. It becomes 'uncommon' or 'uncool' to reveal our emotions and free our inner child when something good (or bad) happens. Over time, we conform.

We become depressed, deserted, and full of uncertainty. We try motivating and pulling ourselves out of whatever hole we fell in, only to slip deeper and deeper into our failures. We have tried wholeheartedly to make everyone else happy, but, in turn, find ourselves lost and desperate for approval. We are full of disbelief and have all but forgotten what it means to be at peace.

Peace, by definition, is: "quiet and tranquility, freedom from disturbance," and it is something I struggled to find for a very long time. The hardest part of growing up and becoming the person we want to be is that no one is preparing us for the storms we encounter along the way.

It never turns out the way we envisioned it would when we were young. Most of us can pinpoint the event that led us down the path we never intended on walking. We visualize ourselves, at that moment, and predict various outcomes of what would have happened if we chose an alternate direction.

Maybe we'd be successful by now, loving our job and the people we surround ourselves with. Maybe we wouldn't feel so isolated, wishing we would've done things differently. Maybe we'd be happy with the life we're living and at peace with our decisions. Some things, however, we just cannot control. The past is the past, and the only thing we can control is our 'now'.

At least that's how it was for me. I was lost in a dark storm and I allowed that darkness to cloud my life for many years. For a long time, I was breathing, but not yet alive. I didn't start living until I no longer allowed that darkness to hinder me from becoming the person I always dreamed of becoming. Sometimes, to find who we are we must lose who we were.

A quest, by definition, is: "a long or arduous search for something." My quest is not nearly as simplistic as that. Yes, it does, indeed, have a beginning, however not yet an end - and it is the in between that defines who I am today and who I will be when the end comes. It has, without a doubt, been long and grueling, but I have finally found what it is I've been searching for… inner peace.

Good For You, Man, So Why Should I Read This Stupid Thing?

I wrote this book for one reason: to serve as a road-map for those searching to live a successful, peaceful, and purpose-filled life. I believe that inner peace is the new success in the world we live in today. All of us are struggling in the crossroads between the kid we used to be and the adult we'd like to be. We all deserve to be happy and live the life we were destined to live - not 'floating around accidental-like on a breeze' as *Forrest Gump* would say.

Contrary to popular belief, our biggest advantage is our

youth. We're not lost in life, we're just early in the process. In case you didn't know, we can actually be whatever we want, whenever we want. Right now, we can try new things and see what we like and don't like. We're too hard on ourselves, in our own minds, to have it all figured out. We need to take what life is giving us and learn how to apply it to what we actually want later on. Once you realize that, the lightbulb turns on. It's like Lindsay Lohan walked in and said, "the limit does not exist."

It will not take as long as you think to drastically change your life, but you must be willing to do so. Inner peace is found just one small step beyond the point where one decides to stop searching for it. If you are determined enough to take another step, the storm will clear and you will find your peace.

You need to understand that success can and will be achieved by trusting in yourself to do exactly what you were put on this earth to do. There's a difference between wishing to be successful and knowing. Those who wish for success, do not truly believe they are capable of achieving it. Those who know, commit to their own definition of success and are relentless in attaining it. The true life test is defining your own meaning of success, and walking the narrow path you've paved for yourself to get there.

A good start to achieving success is finding your **"P.E.A.C.E."** Will we allow our past to alter our present? Or will we decide to find our **P**urpose, **E**scape our past, take **A**ction, **C**hange our autopilot, and become **E**mpathetic to our surroundings?

Yes, for those of you paying attention…those five steps I just listed off spell P.E.A.C.E. See, not as dumb as I look.

The last thing I want is for this to be another sob story you read about a guy who was once lost but now is not. This will be different. Though my story does not have the prestige that the Oprah Winfrey, Mark Cuban, JK Rowling, Jeff Bezos, and Steve Jobs stories do - it will help you better understand who I am, and why I believe I am worthy of helping you.

Yes, I will reference my story, so you can see the process in action, but this will be about you finding peace, and beginning your journey to success. I'll even make you a deal… when you write your own book one day, following your quest, I'll buy a copy and we can share battle wound stories about late night California burritos and peeing off balconies (or whatever).

Sound good?

And so…it begins.

MY ROARING 20'S

"The parties were bigger. The pace was faster, the shows were broader, the buildings were higher, the morals were looser, the liquor was cheaper."
—F. Scott Fitzgerald, The Great Gatsby

On my 20th birthday, I stood on top of my neighbor's car, holding a beer, and then proceeded to pee off the side of it. Oh, did I mention my neighbor was a cop? And the car, I was standing on, happened to have red and blue lights under my feet? What a way to start my Roaring Twenties (sorry, again, Mom).

My 20's were an absolute blast…and mess. You name it, I probably did it. There wasn't a party I missed in college. Between binge drinking, chasing girls far out of my league, and nightly California burritos – you could say I had a roaring good time.

They say a good friend is one who knows all of your stories, but it's the best friend who has lived them with you. Brad, or Edward Cullen (Twilight) as I like to call him, is the guy who lived them with me. Straight out of GQ magazine, the every girl loves me, but I'm actually not a douche about it at all, is how I can best describe Brad. We grew up with very similar backgrounds (minus the popularity he had of course). But, his parents and my parents raised us to be humble and friendly, and we were instantly best friends.

Kevin, your standard 'Converse-wearing Orange County kid', is the guy who taught me about loyalty. He believed that once you're friends with someone, you never turn your back on them. He was funny, mildly attractive (sorry, guy) and loved girls every bit as much as I did. We instantly became best friends, too.

I remember feeling a certain bond with Brad, Kevin, and the rest of my college buddies that I had never felt before. I didn't have very many friends growing up (we'll get to that later), so I made it my mission to know every human I possibly could in college. We did everything together, good and bad.

By some miracle, I managed to make it to my third year at California State University, San Marcos in San Diego, California. Because partying and meeting people had begun to consume my life, school and grades went on the back burner. I had to find ways to work the system if I wanted to stay in school.

Take for example the "Excel, PowerPoint, and Word" assessment requirement that EVERY student had to complete in their first year. I was strolling through campus one day and overheard some faculty discussing how they were going to discontinue the requirement after that year. So, I put in the request for two-time extensions that were given if you had an 'adequate excuse'. Then, I waited it out until they discontinued the requirement and I was exempt from taking it. Talk about perfecting the art of working the system (sorry again, mom and dad).

I manipulated several requirements like that just to ensure I would move on to my junior year at CSUSM. By then, our group of friends were quite popular on campus after the show we put on our first two years. I had rushed ZBT (Jewish fraternity with only one Jew in the entire fraternity) and now had over 30 brothers to call my friends. I made the decision to rush because I felt it was the easiest way to meet new people. I didn't buy into the notion that joining a fraternity was just paying for friends. I believed that the brotherhood those guys shared was something I had not fully experienced yet and was ready to take the next step in my longing for more friends.

I attended mixers with other sororities, fraternity parties, intramural football games, and nearly every social event I possibly could. The problem was that I relied on alcohol to fuel my urge to meet and socialize with as many people as I could. My thought was that I had missed out on many years of having a ton of friends and being social so I was not going to let any more years go to waste. I met every person I possibly could, and I believed the only way to meet those people was to drink and be the life of the party.

No, my grades were not the best they had ever been (not even close), but I now knew everyone on campus. I don't know what switched from when I was younger, but I developed a unique ability to talk to everyone and make friends. I think the difference between myself and the typical "Frat guy" was that for me it didn't matter who you were, I just wanted to know you. I didn't have a motive or affiliation that forced me to only talk to specific groups. I loved talking to everyone.

I developed a passion for people, and that particular

part of me has never changed over the years. I still get a thrill out of meeting someone new and learning something that I didn't know before. Perspective and learning that our way of thinking is not the only way are vital to our growth as humans. Perspective gives us the ability to look at things through the eyes of others and not be consumed with only ourselves. People all around us have a story to tell in which we can maybe learn from, if we care to listen.

I thank my college experience, every day, for teaching me about perspective. I just wish I would've learned earlier that I did not need alcohol to do it.

The Nidal Guys

Through my fraternity in college, I met a few friends along the way (Travis, Kile, Zac and Taylor). They, like Brad and Kevin, became very close friends of mine.

Travis was the guy on campus who everyone knew, and loved. Full of energy, charismatic, and one of the funniest guys I've ever met. We became close friends and quoted every Adam Sandler movie ever made. Kile was your soft spoken, laid back surfer who was full of wit and loved telling Dad jokes with me. He and I immediately understood one another and became close friends, too. Zac (Plaid) was one of the other Rancho kids from my hometown. We nicknamed him Plaid because he was the other surfer who only wore plaid. We didn't know each other well, but he gave me a run for my money and challenged me any chance he got. And then, there was Taylor.

Taylor is the guy who is great at absolutely everything he does (and I hate him for it). He was a semi-professional Wakeboarder, snowboarder, and basically crushed at anything with a board. Competitive, smart, and loved to give me as much sh*t as humanly possible. He is the guy who gave me my nickname in college that people still call me today…*Assclown*. Yes, that's right…my nickname is *Assclown*. If that doesn't paint a picture of how much fun I had in my roaring 20's, I'm not sure what does.

The five of us started a beanie company together called *Nidal Headwear*. Taylor road for *Hyperlite* (a top wakeboard company) so he was well aware of what products were trendy on the market. He knew how to crochet and started designing colorful, intricate beanies for all our friends. To scale, he needed people to sell and sell I could. I told him I could sell a 'ketchup popsicle to a woman in white gloves' (Tommy Boy is the greatest movie ever made). I convinced him to start a full company with the rest of our friends. And just like that, *Nidal* was born.

We had some trouble getting off the ground at first, and needed to find a way to get our name out there. So, how do you organize a space party? You planet…and plan parties I did. It exploded quickly.

We started running party buses periodically to Pacific Beach, downtown Gaslamp, and Padre Stadium to market our brand. Word spread rapidly, and I became pretty good at getting hundreds of (drunk) people out to our events to see our products and party with us. We would set up a table at check-in and began selling 100's of beanies to anyone I could find to come out to our events.

"Dudes, we're selling more than we have in inventory and it's back order city now. What should we do?" I asked in our weekly meeting. That's when we came up with the idea to approach old folk homes and see if they wanted to crochet beanies for us. Hysterical, right? We would take orders from anyone who wanted a beanie and then send it off to the little old ladies who agreed to work for us. It was the perfect business model and ran like clockwork.

We became known as "The Nidal Guys" and I had people contacting me daily for a new beanie or wondering when the next event was. We threw all kinds of cool events. Comedy shows, college nights, bar/club outings, Red Bull Art of Flight premieres, you name it. I once put together an Instagram contest where the person who took the best photo with one of our beanies/stickers won a prize package. We had a chick jump out of an airplane with a *Nidal* sticker on her palm and managed to snap a picture of it (Olivia Johnston, that was legendary).

Things were going well until I selfishly started believing that people only came out for the cool events we were throwing and didn't care about the product. The fact was, and I did not learn this until much later, people appreciated that we created something from scratch and wanted to help us. They only attended our events and partied because that's what we presented to them. We could've put together a charity event or any event really, and they still would've shown support.

Instead, I offered mostly parties, so that's what they did. Once I concluded, in my own selfish way, that people only liked to party - I decided to leave *Nidal* and start my own event coordinating business. So, *Luded Inc.* was born and that brings us to the dawn of the dark days.

The Luded Guys

I remember the first time I stepped foot inside a nightclub. The feeling of that place being so much bigger than myself is something I will never forget. Brad and I stood in the center of *Fluxx Nightclub*, lasers blasting around, the music louder than ever, sparklers going off, and I immediately felt small in a glamorous new world.

"Dude, this is insane," I yelled over the pounding music. "What Maaan? Say it again; I couldn't hear you," he screamed in my ear. "Nothing, never mind...let's go get a drink." I ordered a drink only to look down at a bill that read $18.27. I asked the bartender if it was a mistake and she looked at me and laughed. "Honey, you're in downtown, these are the standard prices," the half-dressed condescending bartender said to me. Who was she to call me honey? Only my Saint Mother had that privilege.

I think that was the defining moment when my mentality shifted. The only thing I wanted to do was conquer that place and gain acceptance of a world I knew absolutely nothing about.

I approached my roommates Brad, Kevin, Scott, and Wags (Matt) with an offer they couldn't refuse. Scott and Wags were your two fitness Gods. They lived at the gym but also loved to have a good time. They were OC kids, well built, good looking, and knew everyone on campus, too. Through my Nidal days, they (along with Brad and Kevin) attended all our events and always supported us.

Yes, I was close with Taylor, Travis and the rest of the "Nidal Guys" but I spent most my time with these degenerates (only kidding, they are all good dudes). Because we were roommates, we did everything together. We lived in a 4-bedroom house a few miles from campus, and I shared a room with Kevin. Though he turned our walk-in closet into his "room" (or 'loveshack" as we liked to call it) for privacy, I honestly believe I saw him naked more than I saw myself naked. I still have nightmares about this.

Even worse than that, our house was NEVER clean. Between five dudes, two dogs, and countless parties, how the hell could it be? I'm fairly confident we did the dishes a total of 7 times the entire time we lived there. We only cleaned when we knew there was a party later that night and there would be girls over. Yeah, it was that bad. I honestly believe you could've gotten a rare disease simply walking in our house. Not to mention, we had a devastating flea infestation. We used to have 'family nights' on Sundays where all the roommates would huddle around the TV to watch *Dexter* only to sit there slapping the fleas off our arms every 2 minutes. When the exterminator finally came out, he told us it was the worst flea infestation he had seen in his 19 years of service. "Good to know Mr. Exterminator Man – maybe we should flee from here…" (see what I did there?)

Anyway, the five of us grew very close. We laughed, respected, and were always loyal to one another. So, they were the guys I trusted and approached with the idea of starting an event coordinating business. My idea was to create a social experience that provided a pipeline for San Marcos students to be INCluded (hence the name Luded Inc.) in the downtown club scene.

The original plan was to do events in clubs and bars until we had enough capital to expand into large-scale festivals and *include* everyone. We had big dreams of bringing a miniature Coachella to the heart of San Diego. What we didn't realize at the time was we would be thrown into a glamorous new world which would be difficult to leave. We and I say "we" but mostly "me", became so consumed with the life that it inevitably ripped apart a bond that five best friends thought could never be broken.

After our successful launch party with 500+ attendees, we made some noise around the city quickly. That catapulted us into gaining contracts at the biggest clubs in the city right out of the gate. Hundreds of kids would come out to our weekly events, and it saddens me to say that partying was at the forefront of our business.

I remember how big it all seemed in the beginning. There we were, five best friends, on a mission to create an event company together, being treated like we were royalty. We suited up together, dressed to impress, and introduced everyone we knew into the downtown party scene. My phone never stopped ringing. I felt like I was on top of the world and had finally made it. People finally wanted something that I had, and it changed me almost immediately.

The kind hearted, happy go lucky kid who treated everyone the same became an arrogant, self-centered "industry guy" who only associated with people who could benefit him in some way or another. I lost everything I knew to be true about myself and had absolutely no idea at the time.

To me, everyone loved me. I mean I was the guy, why wouldn't they? (Cough** "Douche" Cough**). I provided access to a trendy scene where the top DJs and Artists from all over the world came to perform. We went from throwing a few parties here and there to drinking backstage in the VIP lounge with some of the most famous artists in the world.

The five of us became known as "The Luded Guys" and there wasn't a person we didn't know downtown. We talked to everyone. We would make our moves around the city, stopping to interact with any door guy or bottle service girl we could. And boy did I love the glamour. It felt like a scene right out of Great Gatsby.

For me, people finally recognized me. I was finally 'cool.' The problem was, I partied and invested all my time into gaining acceptance from people who cared nothing about me. In the process, I turned my back on the only ones who had been in my corner from the beginning. My five best friends and my family.

Impressing people who I barely knew, with money I didn't have, along with binge drinking, partying and women became a nightly routine for me. I wore expensive clothes, cleaned up nice, and flaunted money around (I surely didn't have) trying to fit in with people who I was never born to fit in with.

It changed me entirely. I became very angry, self-righteous, and viewed the world around me as if it owed me something. I lost my compassion and genuine love for people.

Obsessive, Much?

Around that time, Stacey walked into my life. This is where the steady pace to rock bottom, I was already on, became a spiraling pathway directly to darkness.

She was unlike any girl who had ever come into my life. She was blonde, beautiful, and loved the scene every bit as much as I did. The famous quote from *Blow* with Johnny Depp perfectly describes my relationship with her… "She was beautiful, passionate, and just as crazy as I am…She could party like a man, and love like a woman…"

Though my friends warned me to stay away, I laughed and shut them out completely. I became obsessed with impressing her. We ran around downtown like it was our playground, and I showed her off to anyone I could. We partied backstage with celebrities and spent countless nights out until sunrise. She became my partner in crime, and no one was going to get in our way. She bought into the lies I told her about the rest of the company not pulling their weight, and fed my ego every chance she got.

I continued treating my best friends and partners as if they were beneath me, and eventually, Luded fell apart. Kevin moved away to Australia to travel the world. Scott and I clashed daily, and soon enough, he moved on to a marketing job in Orange County. Brad, Wags and I tried our best to hold it together, but the spark just wasn't there without "The Luded Guys" all working in sequence.

We began to differ on future plans and often argued about the direction we were headed. Between partying, losing my temper daily and treating them like they were beneath me, they lost all trust in me running things. So, I was forced to leave.

I moved in with Stacey shortly after the falling out with my best friends. She was the only person left in my corner once I lost everyone. So, I invested all my time into pleasing her. For the next three years, I became obsessed with making sure she wouldn't leave me, too. We spent every waking moment together, and I shut everyone else out of my life.

The Beginning Of My Own Great Depression

I was lucky enough to land a job at *Pacific Magazine* from the connections I gained through Luded, so at least money was stable. However, the drinking and partying continued. I became more and more depressed every day. Even though we were still going out a bunch, it wasn't the glamour it used to be. There were no more DJ booth tables and VIP rooms with famous artists. I started drinking quite a bit, during the week at home after work, and that's when the clouds started moving in.

I became resentful of everyone and everything. I replayed the chain of events over and over and was still convinced I was right, and everyone else was out to get me. Stacey believed it, too. The thing about her, in which I didn't learn until much later, is she views the world as naturally bad with people in it who only seek to destruct your happiness. I, on the other hand, grew up in a home that taught me to view the world as naturally good and to love your neighbor as yourself. My severe drinking and poor choices, along with her influence, altered my perspective of the way the world works.

I became depressed. I no longer had that spark and ambition in me to want to do great things in this world. I allowed negativity to consume my life. Stacey and I began to fight daily about everything. We fought about my drinking, so I tried as best I could to cut back on that. I attempted at patching things up with the friends I had lost, and then we fought about that because she wanted me to cut them out completely - so I did. I started reaching out to my family and religion again for guidance, but she laughed and said that was pointless - so I stopped that and shut them out, too.

My relationship with my family began to deteriorate because she didn't care for them too much. I lost my job at the magazine because of my lack of focus and motivation, so we fought about money and how I was never going to amount to anything. Because we fought so much, I tried even harder to please her even though I was unhappy with myself and the decisions I was making.

The San Diego Elite

Around that time, I used the last connection I had and reached out to an old bottle service client from the industry, Brian. Brian owned an Internet marketing company (among other businesses), and for a reason I'm still unsure of to this day, he took me under his wing. Though he was quite the partier, Brian quickly became a guy I admired and would do anything for.

He, along with a majority of his buddies, were considered the "San Diego elite." Between fancy dinners, high stakes gambling and dance floor tables at the best clubs, you could say I felt like I was back on top of the world. Things with Stacey settled as she saw the road to luxury was right around the corner if I stayed working with Brian.

So, instead of trying to face my problems head on, I continued running and buried them under a mountain of booze again. I grinded during the week, only to go hard on the weekends with Brian and his friends. I spent countless nights roaming the city in high rise condos until all hours of the evening without a care in the world.

Stacey became convinced I was cheating. I did my best at trying to prove my innocence any chance I got. She didn't believe me though, and our relationship became rocky all over again but to new heights. We screamed and did whatever we could to break each other down. It was awful. I've never spoken to a woman the way I belittled her in some of our fights. I look back now and I am completely disgusted with myself.

I could feel the end nearing with her. My final act of desperation, to save our relationship, was to move us into a new condo. I remember looking at two bedrooms by myself, hoping that it would prove my commitment to starting a family with her. She had no interest in looking at places with me, but I wasn't going down without a fight. I finally found a two-bedroom condo with a loft that I hoped would be the answer to the peace I was longing for.

Unfortunately, it was not.

> *"When you're up, it's never as good as it seems, and when you're down, you never think you'll be up again…but, life goes on."*
> —**Fred Jung, Blow**

AN OLD-FASHIONED AWAKENING

"Maybe you have to know the darkness before you can appreciate the light."
—**Madeline L'Engle**

My parents are old fashioned. They love each other unconditionally and treat one another the way a husband and wife should. I think a big part of them being this way has to do with the fact that neither of them drink, ever. I know, right? How is that even possible? Don't worry, it baffles me, too.

They both came from broken homes in which alcohol was the forefront of their parents' problems, so I'm sure this is the reason my siblings and I were raised in an alcohol-free home. Though there were times I resented them, I look back now and am blessed they did so. I had a peaceful upbringing in which I am very fortunate for today.

As fate would have it, my parents being "old fashioned" resulted in my drink of choice to be just that. Bourbon, two dashes of Angostura bitters, one sugar cube, a few drops of water (maybe), orange peel, topped off with a cherry and I was the happiest (and usually loudest) person in the bar.

I'd approach the bartender with an assured smirk of confidence in which I had developed from years of drinking and would say, "Hey, how ya doin? Old Fashioned, please...bourbon, hold the water." Then I would casually look around to see which fellow bar mates caught a glimpse of my egocentric self ordering what I called "a man's drink." Yeah, real manly I was.

There are several tales as to where the drink originated, but for the most part, the story begins in Louisville, Kentucky. A private social club, called The Pendennis Club, is credited for making the very first old-fashioned (thrillist.com). That seems about right to me. The feeling that came over me every time I drank an Old Fashioned, and met someone else drinking one for that matter, always projected me into a place bigger than myself.

It was as if I had my own social club, with its private set of rules and moral code. I saw others ordering the regular whiskey cokes or vodka sodas and soon developed a smug, almost arrogant, demeanor whenever I ordered mine. Though I was merely in my 20's, I soon believed I was in an elite class of sophisticated gentleman who only drank crafted cocktails built for the privileged. Superrrrrr lame, right?

It amazes me how egotistical I became. There I was, ordering drinks I couldn't afford, trying to impress people I didn't know, just to gain acceptance from guys I admired. Let me tell you something which took me years to figure out. The loudest guy in the room is usually the most insecure. The person flaunting money around is usually the one who doesn't have it. And, the person who claims he has his sh** together and knows everything is almost always lying. The only thing claiming you know everything does is prove you don't know everything. I know this to be true because I was that guy for a long time. But hey, I had to do something to keep my Age of Wonderful Nonsense alive, right?

As it turns out, my parents were right. It almost destroyed my life.

I Hope You Enjoy Being Miserable

"I hope you enjoy being miserable," Stacey mumbled as she walked down the spiral staircase of 'our' remote, isolated loft and inevitably out of my life. That loft resembled striking similarities to the direction I was headed - lonely and isolated, being drawn down a spiraling pathway into an unknown darkness.

There was no use arguing with her, we had done enough of that already. She was right, I was miserable. Between sleepless nights on the couch, a mountain of debt, no real plan for the future, and a severe drinking problem (among other things) - you could say miserable was an understatement.

Miserable, by definition, is: "wretchedly unhappy or uncomfortable; pitiably small or inadequate." The problem with being miserable is the belief that there is no other alternative. You will forever be incapable of achieving success and happiness. This view forces the miserable to act on impulse, seeking quick fixes to end the sadness. Little do we know, these fleeing acts are pushing us further and further down that spiral pathway to darkness.

While I do admit that I wasn't a very pleasant human to be around in those days, she was no peach. She completely broke me down. I hadn't started making the money she'd hoped I would yet, so she used that to destroy my ambition. Instead of encouraging me to grow, she continually reminded me of my flaws and the dreams I hadn't accomplished yet.

I did absolutely everything I could to hold us together. I tried meeting her demands of cutting out friends, not drinking as much, taking vacations, and spending money I didn't have on a new condo for us. She fully consumed me and had control over my happiness entirely. To tell you the truth, she probably should've been gone a lot sooner than that gloomy summer day when she left me in that empty loft.

So, there I was feeling alone again. I stood in that empty house and realized that my entire world just came crashing down. All the pain I had gone through to hold us together resulted in me being the loneliest and most depressed I had ever been.

When we decide to invest all our time into people who care little about us, we no longer recognize what our own happiness looks like. It is important to love and cherish everyone who comes in our life, but we can do this without losing ourselves in the process. Relying on other people for our own happiness will result in our own misery.

So, I did what any broken-hearted twenty something would do - I dove straight into a bottle. I rallied the few friends I had left and partied the pain away. And partied we did. Between Vegas, yacht parties, tables at the best clubs in San Diego, and endless Old Fashions - I did whatever I could to run from the pain. I surrounded myself with people I felt I needed to impress. I tried my best to front that I had it all together and I was happy she was finally out of my life. But, all I was doing was sprinting from my problems and pushing myself further and further down that spiraling pathway to darkness.

A Miracle In The Trenches

Then, one day, my rock bottom came. I stumbled through the entryway of my San Diego condo at O' Dark Thirty on a Sunday. As my footsteps echoed through the vaulted ceilings, I prayed my new roommate didn't wake and see me just getting home from the night before. I have no idea who I was praying to. Not even God himself could have helped me in that current state, and why would he? I was clearly no saint.

I opened the door of my room, quietly, and immediately bolted it behind me. I looked around my empty, lifeless room and began to get the shakes. Sunlight was beaming through the window in the far corner of the room which made me feel more uneasy.

I ran over to the window and closed the shades, hoping

to block the light and calm the shaking. That didn't work. I turned around to reexamine my room. The only thing resembling any sort of life was a full-size bed my cousin Alan had given me because I was too broke to buy my own. It was pushed all the way in the opposite corner of the room sad, and deserted, in its own miserable way.

Laying on the floor next to the bed was a half empty bottle of Jack resting on the Journal my sister had given me for my 26th birthday just a few weeks before. The overwhelming sadness I felt in that moment is something I will never forget. I laid in the corner of my dark room, drowning in my sorrows and cried. It was the first time in my life suicide became an option.

They say in any given year, an American dies by suicide every 12 minutes. This means that roughly 43,000 souls die by suicide every year. *CNN* reported in 2018 that, "Suicide rates increased by 25% across the United States over nearly two decades ending in 2016, according to research published by the US Centers for Disease Control and Prevention. Twenty-five states experienced a rise in suicides by more than 30%... More than half of those who died by suicide had not been diagnosed with a mental health condition…" (Published by Susan Scutti, CNN). Suicide is the 10th leading cause of death in the

United States - and 90% of those who die by suicide have a diagnosable psychiatric disorder at the time of their death. Which means, they could've been saved.

Depression, by definition, is: *'a mental condition characterized by feelings of severe despondency and dejection, typically also with feelings of inadequacy and guilt, often accompanied by a lack of energy and disturbance of appetite and sleep."* It is the helpless, isolated feeling of believing you are never going to amount to anything. The overwhelming feeling of guilt from your past combined with a lack of motivation to do anything for the future seizes control of you.

I was always a happy person, doing my best at laughing and entertaining anyone I could. Though I had a lack of friends growing up, I made up for it in my 20's. I became obsessed with meeting people and having as many friends as I possibly could. Even if it meant doing whatever I had to do to entertain them.

I never thought I would reach a point of overwhelming sadness and defeat. Depression for me, as I'm sure it is for most, was very dark. It didn't become real to me that I was depressed until everyone in my life was gone. I had depended on everyone else to hold me up, and I allowed those people to determine my happiness for me.

As I stood in that room, on the edge of the window looking down at the rocks below, I couldn't believe I had allowed myself to reach the point of total destruction. I remember thinking, how did I get here? How could someone who was so confident that life would bring so much joy be in a position to end his life?

Then, the miracle came.

I opened the journal and found the letter my sister had written me for my birthday. That letter saved me from taking my own life that day. I read it, over and over again, and realized that someone out there saw the good in me. She is the reason I'm here today and she saved me from the darkest place I've ever been.

That was the day I began my Peace Quest.

It's Quite Rocky Down Here

You don't fully understand what rock bottom is until you're looking out the window of your empty, lifeless room, deciding if it's worth it to even be alive anymore. There's a certain emptiness we all must feel in which inspires us to do better in this world. I'm sad to say I found that emptiness... but am lucky enough now to understand that I'm better than that depressed, lost version of myself.

I believe we do not fully understand who we are until

we become someone we are not. I had become the person who I never wanted to be, but, on that day, decided it was time to become the person I was born to be.

"Today is the day I hit my rock bottom. I have found myself in the worst place I have ever been and I no longer know who I am anymore. I am $80,000 in debt. My health is slowly deteriorating from the years of partying and neglect. I have betrayed and lost almost every friend and love who has come into my life. I can feel my family slipping away. I have told others and myself so many lies over time where I finally have no grasp over what the truth is and isn't anymore. I think you finally get to the point I'm at in my life when you've been running so fast and for so long that you can no longer stand on your own two feet anymore. It's time for me to stop running. I'm ready to acknowledge the fact that I have some serious problems that have forced me to hate everything about myself and who I am today. No more hiding. No more faking. No more lying. No more partying. No more sulking. No more blaming others. No

more putting myself down. No more excuses. No more trying to be someone I am not. Today I start the journey of depending on myself to be the person I've always dreamed of becoming. Today, I start the journey of finding myself again. Today I start believing in myself again. Today, I begin my quest to finding Peace." – August 3, 2016

So, what did the fish say when he ran into a wall? "Dam." And Damn is right…I ran straight into that wall.

If you're here reading this, however, I have some good news for you… I climbed over that 'damn' metaphorical wall and peace was waiting on the other side. Though I do not wish it upon anyone, we all must feel some sort of pain in our lives before we experience a breakthrough into finding peace and purpose for being here.

I'll never forget that day when my rock bottom came. It was on that day when I had nothing in my life to hope for and only myself to blame for it. But, as J.K Rowling put it, "rock bottom became the solid foundation on which I rebuilt my life."

PURPOSE – STEP 1

"The purpose of life is not just to be happy. It is to be useful, to be honorable, to be compassionate, to have it make some difference that you have lived and lived well..."

—Ralph Waldo Emerson

You will not find Peace until you find Purpose.

I started on my quest with little knowledge of what my Purpose was and how I was going to find it. I was lost. The only thing I knew about my life were all the things I hated about it. My initial thought, torch it. But, saner minds prevailed.

Purpose, by definition, is: "the reason for which something is done or created...or for which something exists." We all need purpose. Living without a sense of purpose is not living at all. Whatever your craft may be, we all have the urge to be useful in some way or another. Living as though we are making no difference in the world will only lead us to unhappiness. Understanding what your purpose is and why you are here will bring a fulfilling clarity to your life.

"Ready To Fix It" List

Though most self-help books I read told me to start with the things that are positive about my life and areas where I had found success - I started with the negative, and it worked for me. I wrote out everything I did not like about myself so I could see how bad it really was on paper. I know, poor me, right? Yes, it was painful. Yes, it brought out things I knew and did not know about myself. And yes, it was one of the hardest things I've ever done. But I did it. And no, I am certainly not proud of this list (sorry again, Mom).

I don't like that I drink

I don't like that I do drugs

I don't like that I smoke cigarettes

I don't like how much weight I've gained

I don't like how cynical I've become

I don't like how much I lie to people

I don't like how unmotivated I am

I don't like my job and how empty it is

I don't like being broke and pretending to be rich

I don't like how much money I spend on unimportant things

I don't like the people I surround myself with

I don't like trying to please people that genuinely do not care about me

I don't like that I haven't found my direction and purpose yet

I don't like wasting time and walking around aimlessly

I don't like setting plans/goals and then not following through with them

I don't like being unorganized

I don't like how much I cuss and how I speak to people

I don't like that I have lost my compassion and empathy

I don't like who I am as a person today...

...But, I'm ready to fix it.

Sitting on the floor in my empty, dark room and writing out those problems on paper was one of the best things I ever did. I could finally see what I was running from for so many years. At that moment in time, I didn't quite see the light at the end of the tunnel, but I knew I wasn't defeated. Yes, I was miserable. And yes, those problems were bad - but not bad enough to where they couldn't be fixed. Rather than sit there and lie to myself about making drastic changes overnight, I just decided to be realistic.

On that day, I vowed to make small changes every day to better myself. I knew it could not be done all at once, but I could commit to taking small steps every day. I did not want to party, and I wanted to be honest with myself and others. I wanted to work hard and make a difference in this world. I wanted to make my family smile again. I wanted to make myself smile again. That day I made a promise to fix those problems, one step at a time. That's all I could promise at the time, but one thing's for certain - I was going to change, and I was going find the best version of myself.

We're only on this earth for a short time, and I was no longer going to waste it by worrying about people and things that did not matter. The only thing I could do at that moment was promise myself to put my head down and work until I no longer felt pain. I told myself I would be successful and would one day not hurt anymore. It was time to rebuild. It was time to find happiness and peace in myself again. So, I began the journey to finding my purpose.

The Whole God Thing

Now that I had a basic understanding of the things I did not like about myself, it was time to figure out how I was going to fix them. One day I walked into a thrift store with my brother and sister and I came across Rick Warren's, "The Purpose Driven Life" tucked away in the countless used books they carried. If I'm being completely honest (because I guess that's what I do now) I actually came across the book twice.

The first time I glanced over it and remember thinking, "Yeah man, some purpose would be real nice right about now but who has 40 days…other than that weirdo Noah who built an ark." Then I continued looking around as if nothing happened. It wasn't until I came across the book a second time on the last shelf when I realized that somebody out there was trying to tell me something.

For me, I did not fully grasp what my purpose was until I picked up that book and gave the whole God thing a shot. I came to find that, all this time, I had a teammate standing by ready to help me figure my life out. Yes, I may lose some of you here with the whole God thing which you may not believe in – but, for the *purpose* of this chapter (see what I did there), can you just humor me for a minute? When you write your own book one day, you can use your own God (and I'll gladly read it), but for now, let me use mine... Thanks, gang.

Let me begin by saying you can believe whatever you want to believe to help find your purpose in this life. Though Mr. Big Chief upstairs did help me, I'm certainly not going to sit here and tell you my way is the only way.

I think we all need to believe there is something out there bigger than ourselves that drives us to become the person we always wanted to be. It's a certain hope that forces us to do better.

Some people find their hope in religion – others in meditation, yoga, underwater basket weaving, fishing, badminton, success - you name it. Still, others believe there is no higher being and are perfectly able to build their own moral code to live by. I don't disagree or have an opinion as to where people should find their hope or what they should believe because that isn't for me to decide. We're all walking our own path and should believe whatever we need to in which inspires us to be hopeful for a better tomorrow.

As my new buddy Rick put it, "We all need hope to cope..." For me, I found my hope in God. It was that hope that would guide me along through this process, and I needed to understand that it all started with the big chief upstairs. So, I began my 40-days of Purpose.

"Today, not only did I buy 'The Purpose Driven Life' and start my 40-days to finding purpose, but I also went back to church. It's difficult for me to describe the feeling that came over me as I walked in that door. The only word that comes to mind is a sense of peace. I was welcomed, not overwhelmed. I was looked in the eye by peaceful people who only showed compassion without knowing my story at all. The theme of my day today was peace, purpose, and compassion and I haven't felt any of those in a long time. When I got home, I saw some pictures and videos of Stacey out partying, and in all honesty, it hurt quite bad. I thought about crawling into my bed and hiding from the world, but then I remembered how I felt when I walked in that

place today. I started thinking positively again. My journey of recovery has begun, and its time I find my soul again. Yes, she will continue to hurt me in ways I didn't know possible, but the only thing I can do is focus on bettering myself as a person. I realized today that I am incapable of changing her and others, but I am capable of changing myself. That is my mission. Excited for change and what God has planned for my life. My future happiness and purpose are beginning to feel closer than ever..."

I think religion gets a bad rap. People view religion as this type of perfect entity you must be, the God you must bow down to, or the judgmental person you must become. Religion isn't about the wars, anger, and judgment that come out of it in extreme situations. There are extremes in anything you believe. Religion is about believing in something that gives you hope to fight the daily battles of life.

It means you can walk into an environment where you were so unhopeful and sad with nowhere to turn, and instantly feel at ease. You walk in a door, and something hits you that you've never felt before. You don't have a worry in the world in that moment. You're surrounded by people who simply smile at you. They didn't question where I had been, who I was, where I worked, how much money I made, if I had done drugs or drank alcohol. All they said was, "Hey, how are you today? We're glad you're here."

We can't shun people for turning to religion in times when all else has failed. In any walk you're on, we always need something to strive for that's bigger than ourselves. For some people, that something is believing in a certain God to get them through. It forces us to be better people, giving us something to hope for. This provides us with a sense of purpose and reason to keep on living. And that's a beautiful thing.

If I woke up every morning and didn't have to make my bed, go to work, or live my life, what would I do? What would my purpose be? What defines woke up and live my life? It's defined by what my culture has taught me. What we understand and 'know to be true' is based entirely on what we've been taught and heard from other people. We need to make our own decisions. We need to rely on our own outlook and understanding of the way the world works. We need to gain our own perspective, draw our own conclusions, and then give back what we've learned in a peaceful way.

I think we all take in the same information and feel a different way about it. What we need to learn to do is take in that information and express it in a way that isn't forcing our opinion onto others. I believe what I believe because it gave me hope when I had nothing left to hope for. That doesn't mean I now feel the urge to force my opinion onto others. I think people should believe in whatever they need to help get them through the daily battles they are fighting within themselves. If that means believing in a certain religion, or God, then who am I to tell them they're wrong for doing so?

I was lost for a long time and spent years doing a lot of terrible things. The truth is, I wouldn't be where I'm at today unless I went through everything that I did. I think if I didn't experience all the pain I did along the way, I wouldn't have the unique understanding and perspective I do now. I lived to talk about those problems, so that's a miracle all in itself. I cannot hide from my past, the only thing I can do is learn to use it for good.

I continued with the 40-day Purpose Driven Life with a new found open mind and energy. I learned that there were many things in my past I was driven by including guilt, resentment, fear, materialism, need for approval, etc. and it was time I stopped allowing those things to alter my life. It was time to find the true passion that drove me.

Find The Passion That Drives You

To do this next part of my Peace Quest I needed some help. And for those of you still worried I'm going to cram Jesus down your throat, fear no more. We're taking a break from the lessons I learned from the big guy upstairs and shifting our focus.

Most of the people who were still close to me had already gathered that I was doing some soul searching and on my way to bettering my life. So, when I asked them for a little help with my quest they were more than willing to reach out a hand. Along with The Purpose Driven Life book that I was reading, I decided to read *Three Feet From Gold* by Sharon L. Lechter and Greg S. Reid (yeah, all of the sudden I figured out how to read).

I wanted to learn everything there was to know about being successful and bettering my life. This book, based on the teachings of Napoleon Hill, taught me about passion. It tells a story of a guy who is struggling with his business, behind on his rent, has a girlfriend who leaves him, and is distracted by all the failures around him (pretty sure he wrote the book about my life, but don't quote me on that). Through his trials, he gains a new perspective about believing in yourself to control your destiny. Pretty inspiring, right?

So, I got to work. I asked three people who I believed knew me the best (my Mom, Brad, and my cousin Alan) to write ten things (jobs, if you will) they thought I could do, on one side of a piece of paper. Then, on the other side, ten things they thought I was good at. Basically, passion on one side, talent on the other.

Those who say you cannot allow passion to influence your life and career decision have it completely backward. Passion is what drives all of us to do great things. All dreams begin with a dreamer, and within that dreamer resides a passion limitless beyond what we believe to be capable of.

I did not allow the opinions of others to skew me away from completing this step. This step alone was vital to finding my purpose and I wasn't going to allow negative people to influence my life anymore. I chose people in my life who had stood by me through it all and knew almost everything there was to know about me, collectively.

I chose my mother because, well, after 32 hours of labor she deserved to be in the mix. And because I learned at a young age that life doesn't come with a manual, it comes with a mother. Even though she didn't know the extent of my problems and all of the terrible things that I had done, she had a pretty good idea of the person she raised. Everything she didn't know, Brad and Alan knew - so they filled in the gaps. I didn't reveal that I had asked others to compile a list to any of the three people because I wanted their opinions to be completely honest and not skewed in any way.

After I had asked them to complete that list, I began working on the list myself. I wrote out the things that I was passionate about, and enjoyed, and everything started to fall into place.

My List

Passion (Jobs)	Talent (Character Traits)
1. Helping people (Counseling)	1. Serving
2. Motivating People (Life Coach)	2. Motivating
3. Event Coordinating	3. Selling
4. Coaching Baseball	4. Empathizing
5. Teaching	5. Leading
6. Serving People (Talent Agent)	6. Negotiating
7. Writing	7. Coaching
8. Public Speaker (Motivational)	8. Problem Solving
9. Comedian (Dad Jokes)	9. Speaking (Communicating)
10. Sales/Real Estate	10. Commanding a Room

Please note that the Passion and Talent side are on opposite sides of the paper and are not necessarily supposed to correlate with each other in numerical order. Just write out all of your passions on one side, and then all of your talents on the other without flipping the paper back and forth to see what you wrote. It will turn out more authentic this way.

Even in my darkest of times, I was still able to find the things that I am most passionate about and that excite me. I asked myself questions like, "What can I do with my time that makes me happy," or "If money didn't exist, would I still get up and do what I'm about to do today?" These are the questions that matter. The trick was not focusing on money or what others thought about what I became. I just allowed myself to write down the things that made me the happiest.

However, I did find myself in a place where I believed I was not talented at anything. I compared myself to the successes of others and beat myself up quite a bit. I had always believed that I would be successful one day, but comparing myself to others resulted in putting myself down. I had just been misguided and told myself that I was not worthy of doing the things I loved and being the person I wanted to be. That stopped right there. I no longer focused on them and looked within.

That list took me a long time but I did not leave my loft until I forced myself to think about the areas in my life where I had found some success. Even though it was a very minute amount of triumph, I, at least, had a few areas where I excelled at certain things. Call them 'small wins' if you will.

Simply writing out my own list allowed me to see a trend in the things that excited me the most - serving people. I was anxious to see what the people who were closest to me came up with as well, and to my surprise, the results were quite similar.

Brad's List (For Me)

Passion (Jobs)	Talent (Character Traits)
1. Counseling	1. Speaking
2. Serving	2. Selling
3. Client Handling	3. Convincing your opponent
4. Public Speaking	4. Leading
5. Teaching	5. Commanding a Room
6. Sales (Any)	6. Negotiating
7. Event Management	7. Problem Solving
8. Lawyer	8. Finding Solutions
9. Doctor	9. Emphasizing
10. Plumber	10. Work Ethic

Mom & Dad List (For Me)

Passion (Jobs)	Talent (Character Traits)
1. Teaching	1. Personal Communication
2. Coaching	2. Compassion
3. Christian Talent Agent	3. Helping People
4. Event Planning	4. Communication/Skills with all ages
5. Helping People	5. Determination
6. Mentor	6. perseverance
7. Counselor	7. Motivating People
8. Social Worker	8. Listening
9. Athletic Psychologist	9. Understanding
10. TV Host	10. Overcoming Obstacles

Alan List (For Me)

Passion (Jobs)	Talent (Character Traits)
1. Sell the sh*t out of something	1. Talking to people
2. Tour Guide	2. Making connections
3. Resort Manager	3. Realizing people's needs
4. Guest Relations Manager	4. Entertaining People
5. Talent Agent	5. Sharing Charisma

It amazed me how similar the lists were. I immediately began to see what my purpose was for being here. It was now time for me to combine them. I took the top 10 things from each side of all lists that either overlapped or that I felt best represented me. Then, I eliminated any of the ones that I felt did not fit or did not define me the best.

For example, Brad (as clever as he is) thought it would be funny to throw in plumber even though he knows I have no idea how to fix a broken pipe. For you plumbers out there, I have some serious respect for you though. Without you I couldn't poop or shower - so, for that, I thank you.

Some things I eliminated relatively quickly, but others were a bit more challenging. But, I did it.

Final Combined List

Passion (Jobs)	Talent
1. Serving People	1. Serving/Helping People
2. Motivator/Public Speaker (Life Coach)	2. Motivating
3. Event Coordinating	3. Speaking (Communicating)
4. Counseling	4. Networking
5. Teaching & Coaching	5. Emphasizing
6. Writer	6. Leading
7. Athletic Psychologist	7. Negotiating
8. Social Worker	8. Commanding a Room
9. Real Estate	9. Entertaining People
10. Guest Relations (Resort Director)	10. Problem Solving

Now that I had my final list of ten, the fun started. I could see, on paper, what my passions were and the areas where I had found some success in my life. So, I put it all together. Little by little I narrowed it down to one passion and one talent until I found my purpose. The trends I saw in my list allowed me to combine several items off both sides into one purpose.

Take, for example, my talent side. I noticed right away that I was good at helping people by motivating, communicating, emphasizing, leading, networking and problem-solving. Throw in some entertainment with my annoying Dad jokes, and you could say I found what I was talented at fairly quickly. Yeah sure, 'commanding a room' and 'negotiating' were cool, but I remember using those abilities in my past to manipulate people. So, I stayed away from those. Once I knew what I was talented at, I flipped the paper over and began finding the passion and job that could combine all of those.

This step didn't happen in one sitting. It took a bit of research to fully make my decision on what I wanted to do for the rest of my life. Although Guest Relations Director at a resort would be quite entertaining, I opted to not go that direction after looking into a bit. In addition, a Social Worker and Athletic Psychologist would require more schooling and we all know what happened last time I went to college… so that was out of the question.

Long story short, I came to the conclusion that I was

called to serve and motivate people to better their lives. After everything I had been through, I had a certain understanding and revelation that some never find. That made it my duty to share it with the world in hopes of saving at least one person from the empty place I found myself in. I would now make it my mission to serve people by becoming a writer, motivator, keynote speaker, and life coach.

There you have it - I found my purpose. The clarity and overwhelming happiness that struck me in that moment is something I will never forget. I was home alone and I stood up in that empty loft looking over at that spiraling staircase and screamed, "IT'S NOT OVER YET, I'VE ONLY JUST BEGUN."

Yes, it was a cheesy line that I picked up from *Happy Gilmore* but that's okay. I don't care. I love cheese and it was my moment. And even cheese all by itself is still ProvALONE – so, HA to all you critics out there.

Mark Twain said, "The two most important days in your life are the day you are born and the day you find out why." I was at the point where I found my why, now it was up to me. It was right then when I realized my journey had only just begun.

I believed in myself to find my purpose, and I did. I fixed my mind on that purpose and could now see myself walking the path and being that person. It would allow me to finally use my love for people and ability to interact with others in a positive light. I believe that if you can visualize it, you can be it…you just have to imagine that you're already doing it.

My mission on this quest was not simply to survive but to come alive through passion, purpose and ultimately peace. I was now one step closer to finding that peace and becoming the person I always dreamed of becoming.

> *"Tell the world what you intend to do but first show it."*
>
> **—Napoleon Hill**

Part One - Purpose

1. What don't you like about yourself?
    1. List out of all the things you are unhappy about with your life right now
    2. Do not hold back, EVERY single thing
    3. Hold onto the list, we will reference back to it

2. What do you like?
    1. What are your interests? What makes your heart sing? What would you do if money didn't matter?
    2. What are you talented at? What are the areas in your life where you found some success?

3. Find The Passion That Drives You (Passion/Talent List)
    1. Ask three people to write 10 things they think you could do, on one side of a piece of paper. Then, on the other side, ten things they think you're good at. Passion on one side, talent on the other.
    2. Complete the list yourself
    3. Narrow the combined lists down to 1 and 1

4. Reevaluate your lists
    1. We need to be certain your purpose is in some way serving this world. Ask yourself how you want to be remembered
    2. Is it something you are willing to teach others and would like to spend more time doing it?
    3. It needs to also be something different than the things you have done that were negative in the past. This doesn't mean an immediate job change and completely new course (though it can mean this). This means a new perspective on the way you were doing things before. Now view the world as if you are serving it

5. Fix your mind
    1. Beginning steps in visioning yourself serving and carrying out this purpose
    2. Morning vision and rehearsed purpose
    3. Believe in yourself and see yourself walking the path

If you'd like to begin your own Peace Quest, you can find the Ebook with worksheets and a detailed plan to The Five Steps of Finding Purpose on the website www.ThePeaceQuest.com

ESCAPING YOUR PAST – STEP 2

"The best way to escape from the past is not to avoid or forget it but to accept and forgive it."

—Unknown

You will not find Peace until you learn how to Escape Your Past.

"Welcome to Jack in the Box, how can I help you?"

"Hi…" I tragically mumbled into the drive thru speaker for the third time that week. "Can I have four tacos with no sauce and a few salt packets."

"Sure. That'll be $2.13 at the first window please."

What a joke. Where else can you get a full meal with legendary taste and superhero-like powers that instantly cure a God-Awful hangover for only $2.13? Jack in the

Box was my knight in shining armor and I, for sure, needed rescuing.

That day was just like any other day. I woke up around 1 pm after a long night and early morning of partying my life away. Everything hurt, my head especially, but I had perfected unique coping methods on how to handle my frequent hangovers. I would climb out of bed (stumbling usually) and make my way to the hopefully filled Britta in the fridge. Let me tell you... the moment you take that first sip of cold water after a long night of heavy drinking, it feels as if you are drinking from God's personal pond.

From there, I'd begin to assess the severity of how bad my decisions were the night before. I'd reread the drunken texts I sent out to every human in my contacts – and immediately followed up by sending a few necessary apologies. Then, it was more water, Advil, and time to figure out how much money I had left to buy food. I had a serious case of 'the funds are low' because I usually spent all my money trying to impress people the night before. I was the true definition of going broke trying to act rich.

My finances were an absolute mess. Save money? What does that even mean? It was my Roaring 20's, what could possibly go wrong... (Hmm, a Great Depression, maybe?). I had spent years partying and neglecting my bank account entirely because I was terrified of what I would find. I'm not kidding. I made it a point to pay as little attention as possible to where my money was going and the amount of debt I was in. I remember countless weekends of spending thousands of dollars out at the club, only to wake up the next morning counting quarters to buy four tacos at Jack in the Box. I ran like this for years.

So, after I found the quarters I needed, it was time to make my way to my personal savior – Jack. I pulled up only to find "that guy" with his engine shut off taking decades to order. There are two kinds of people in this world... Those who shut their engine off in the drive thru line (sociopaths) and those who do not (normal humans). Please pick a side. Anyway, after beating my wheel and blasting my horn at the guy to hurry up, I finally ordered.

It amazes me the little thought I gave to others and their own struggles in my drinking days. The only thing I cared about was biting into that taco, instantly curing my terrible decisions of the night before. When the window clerk handed me that bag, it was as if I came down the stairs on Christmas morning and the little red bike was there waiting for me.

Disgusting, I know. And no, not just the tacos, me in general. I look back now and I hate that person. Not only was I dead broke and an asshole to others, I was also severely overweight. I ate terribly, drank religiously, and never exercised. Perfect combo, right? I would sweat walking upstairs, so the elevator and I became the best of friends. But, like that elevator, I've had my ups and downs (I know you like that one).

As you know, I finally decided to change my life and am now the happiest I've ever been. I went from being 254lbs, angry at the world, and hating myself – to a healthy 200lbs, ambitious to serve this world, and at peace with who I am. That lost twenty something who lacked any sort of motivation and direction became committed to finding the best version of himself and living out his purpose. I won't sit here and sugarcoat it either... it was the hardest thing I've ever done. But I did it, and I guarantee you can too if you're determined enough to do so.

Escape, by definition (seeing a trend here), is: "an act of breaking free from confinement or control..." Notice how this says 'breaking free,' and not 'forgetting all together' or 'completely avoiding.' We all have pasts in which I'm sure we are not proud of (I know I do), but it's what we do with our pasts that will define our future.

We all need to learn how to open up about our pasts so it can lead us to freedom.

Learning To Let Go

"OW, SH*T that hurt," I yelled as my roommate Chuck attempted to pop my now excruciating broken shoulder back into place. Chuck, or "Dad" as I like to call him, is one of the smartest, hardworking and funniest guys I have ever met. We met in college, and he landed a job with a distinguished private equity firm in La Jolla a few miles from where I lived. He needed a place closer to work, and I needed someone who had their sh*t together to move in after the ex left. So, he became my guy.

We were both, in our infinite wisdom, convinced that my shoulder was only dislocated and could easily be popped back into place. After watching our fair share of YouTube videos on the subject, we were now experts. Everything we read and watched told us that I would know, with certainty, if my shoulder was broken. It would be an unbearable amount of pain they said. So, we decided it would be a good idea to just pop it back in place to avoid a hospital visit. Worst idea I've ever had. We shot the bone straight up and I've never felt more pain in all my life.

When I arrived at the hospital and took x-rays, the doctor immediately came in and said, "Ryan, how much pain are you in? I was under the impression that you dislocated your shoulder based on your relaxed state, but this is a severely bad break. You must be in a lot of pain." He was indeed right. But I had learned how to hide my pain with years of practice. "I mean yeah, chief, that's why I'm here. How do we fix this thing in case I need to be the shoulder for someone to cry on one day…" See, told you, these Dad jokes are never ending.

You see, I had developed an abnormally high tolerance for pain over the years. Not just physically, especially with the new chip on my shoulder, but emotionally as well. I used humor to mask my pain so people didn't have to feel sorry for me. I would shrug it off (well, not in that moment – shrugging would not have been a good idea) like it wasn't a big deal how much pain I was in, only to bury myself deeper into my issues.

I'm not, by any means, proud of my past. But it's there, and I can't avoid it. Sure, I tried masking my pain by putting myself down for others to laugh at my expense - but it got me nowhere. I constantly joked to other people about how fat and broke I was as if it didn't bother me at all. I lied to people and told them it was everyone else's fault for my business failures, break-ups, and problems. I told people whatever I could to get them to look away from my unbearable pain.

Running so fast and for so long resulted in me being the most depressed I have ever been. I didn't begin to feel at ease with my past until I stopped running, took responsibility for my actions, and learned how to accept the things I could not change.

We are taught responsibility at a young age. 'Take out the trash… In bed by 9:00 p.m. …do your homework, etc.' I may have hated it at the time, but it has shaped my ability to accomplish things later in life. The problem with responsibility (and being an adult) is no one tells you that you'll have to do things on your own one day without someone telling you to do them.

For most of my life, I've had someone determining my next move for me. Whether it be a parent, teacher, coach, friend, girlfriend, etc., I've always depended on someone to push me along. And because of that, they were the first people I blamed when things went south.

When I made the decision to become fully dependent on myself, to be the person I wanted to be, I stopped blaming individuals and circumstances for my actions and took responsibility for them. It was then when I began to be at peace with my past. I started making decisions for myself, not on impulse and not influenced by what people wanted me to do. As my old pal Rick Warren said it, "At some point in your life, you must decide whether you want to impress people or influence people…" I opted for the latter.

For this next step in my quest, it was time for me to learn how to let go. To fix a broken soul, all you need is Hope. The troubling thing about hope is that it usually appears in times of pure desperation. When we have nothing else to turn to and our backs against the wall, it is hope that gets us through. Hope for a better tomorrow. Hope for happiness and peace in an empty world. Hope is powerful. It is the genuine belief that no matter what life throws at us, we will overcome it. Hope has gotten me through the darkest of times, and there isn't a day that goes by now where I am not hopeful for a better tomorrow. I needed hope for this next step because it helped calm the storm within so I could escape my past.

What's Your Story?

The very first step in escaping my past was to tell one person my story. It had to be the absolute truth - no holding back. I thought about it a lot and wanted it to be someone who was close to me. Someone who had at least a basic understanding of the things that went on in my life. This was different than what anyone had told me to do. Apparently, there were numerous people out there who studied for years on how to treat my problems.

We learned that from Tommy Boy... "You know, a lot of people go to college for seven years...yeah they're called doctors." Not that I have any objection to seeing a psychiatrist because I believe they help hundreds of thousands of people every single day- I just did not have the money to do so. Nor did I feel comfortable talking about my problems with someone who didn't know me.

I chose Brad, and it worked for me. Yes, he had been there through it all and had witnessed my struggles first hand, but there were things he didn't know. It felt amazing to get everything out in the open and finally tell the truth about all my problems. As we spoke, things came out a lot easier than I expected. I revealed to him where my problems began, where I was at now, and everything in between. I confessed to all of the lies I had told him and myself over the years and expressed my new found hope in my broken world.

He accepted my many apologies and said that I needed to feel the pain before I could find my peace. He went on further to tell me that he always believed in me to be the person I wanted to be, but that I needed to be able to believe in myself to be that person. He said I never needed anyone to show me what was right - my problem was that I just looked to everyone else to tell me before looking within. He expressed how excited he was to see the heights of where I would go now that I was fully letting go of my past.

What a guy, right? After I told my story to someone without holding back, I started to feel at ease with getting everything off my chest. Escaping my past was getting closer than ever. I recommend you do the same if you're holding onto things in which you don't know how to let go of. If you don't have a Brad, call me and I'll gladly listen to your story. I'm free these days anyway, it's not like I'm out at the bar anymore ;)

Hurt Locker

The next thing I did was make a list of every single person that I had hurt over the years and what I did to hurt them. Yes, this is straight out of the 12-step program, but it helped me drastically. The list was quite long. But once I could see it written down on paper, it was easier to work on reaching out and making things right. It made me feel a lot better about myself once I made things right with the people I had hurt over the years. I no longer had that hanging over my head.

As I went down my list and began contacting these people, some did not accept my apology or want anything to do with me. They rejected me. But, that was okay with me. I acknowledged that I had a rough past and the only thing I could do was work on a better future. I told them I was sorry for the things done to hurt them and that I understood why they felt that way. I knew I would walk a lonely path, but those who stuck with me would always be by me. I did not argue with any of these people about the things they or I did. We can only be responsible for our own path. We need to let others have theirs.

Have You Learned Your Lesson?

The last step in escaping my past was knowing that all of the things I had been through in my life prepared me for who my future self would be. I came to the understanding that darkness clouded my life so that I could, in turn, find the light. As Meryl Streep would say, it was time to "take your broken heart and make it into art…"

I wrote down all the major life lessons I had been taught over the years through my pain so I could begin sharing them with others. Back to my buddy Rick on this one, "While it is wise to learn from experience, it is wiser to learn from the experience of others…Imagine how much needless frustration could be avoided if we learned from each other's life lessons."

Though I was ashamed of my problems, I decided to write them out so I could share them with people one day in hopes of maybe helping someone. This was probably the toughest part of escaping my past, but like all of the others, it had to be done.

Luckily, I had already written down the things I did not like about myself, so that made it a little easier to complete this lesson list:

1. *Be a leader, not a follower (thanks for this one, Dad).*
2. *We all must feel pain in our lives before we experience a breakthrough into finding peace and purpose*
3. *We do not fully understand who we are until we become someone we are not*
4. *If we do not focus on the tunnel, we'll inevitably find the light.*
5. *Do not wish to be successful, know with certainty you will be. Know exactly what it is you want and be determined to get just that*

6. *Possessions and material objects can vanish at any moment, but the ones you love are always with you*

7. *We all need Hope to Cope*

8. *Trying to impress people with money you do not have, along with drinking and partying, will result in an unbearable emptiness forcing you to lose your compassion and genuine love for people.*

9. *Being in a toxic relationship will leave you isolated and miserable*

10. *Manipulating people for your own benefit will leave you all but alone*

11. *To drastically change your life, you must make drastic changes in your life*

12. *Believe in yourself to make the right decisions and put yourself in a situation to make moral decisions*

13. *You cannot be great without a reason. Find your why*

14. *You're the only one standing in your own way*

15. *Don't Conform. Transform*

I sat up in that loft and said to myself, "Damn, I guess I have learned a lot over the years. Here I thought I was just a giant idiot with no value to give the world." I reread the list over and over and each time I did, it sent me back to the place where I learned that particular lesson. I knew I could not change my past, but I could take what I had learned and use it to better my future and the lives of others. I learned how to escape from the past not by avoiding or forgetting it - but by accepting and forgiving it. Though the pain of my past brought an ugly shame, I learned to accept my weaknesses and use them to help others avoid them.

We all have pasts we are not proud of. If we decide to dwell on the past, it will negatively affect our future. We need to take those things and learn to use them for the good of the World. Our own perspective and understanding of the way the world works are meant to be shared so we can help people avoid the mistakes we made along the way. It is vital to our progression as humans. Letting go of your past and freeing yourself of those burdens will clear your mind. It will allow you to move forward and begin carrying out your new-found purpose.

I now had a clean slate. I had found my purpose and escaped my past so I could start to live the life I always wanted. It was time to take action and build a plan.

"Where the determination is, the way can be found."
—**George S. Clason, The Richest Man in Babylon.**

Part Two - Escaping Your Past:

1. Tell One Person Your Story
    1. The absolute truth, no holding back
    2. Someone close to you has a basic understanding of everything so they might be the right choice.
    3. It does not matter who the person is, just as long as it's the complete truth

2. Hurt Locker
    1. Make a list of every single person you have hurt and what you did to hurt them
    2. Once you have it on paper, begin reaching out to make things right
    3. Prepare for rejection and hurt
    4. Do not argue and present your case. Simply apologize and tell them you are working to better your life
    5. The second part of Hurt Locker is to assess who has hurt you, if the relationship can/should be fixed, and if that person encourages you to grow.

3. Lesson List
    1. Write down all of the major life lessons you have learned and when you learned them.

2. Know and understand that all the things you have been through prepared you for what's to come.

If you'd like to begin your own Peace Quest, you can find the Ebook with worksheets and a detailed plan to The Steps of Escaping Your Past on the website www.ThePeaceQuest.com

ACTION – STEP 3

"The path to success is to take massive, determined actions... A real decision is measured by the fact that you've taken a new action. If there's no action, you haven't truly decided."

—Tony Robbins

You will not find Peace until you take massive, determined Action.

Gazing out the window of my isolated office in the consulting firm I now worked for, I began thinking about how miserable I was. I had spent the past year battling the worst depression I have ever experienced. I was bouncing around from job to job avoiding the purpose I had spent so many months searching for. I was worn out. I had been clinging to old ways of doing things, allowing past business failures and relationships to keep me from pursuing my dreams. I was sitting in a job I hated, living a life that was not only destroying my ambition - but most of all, my heart.

Then something hit me. I thought about all the progress I had made over the past year. I had lost 175 pounds (50 of my own, 125 in toxic relationship form). I had begun writing again and found the purpose and passion that drove me. Though I was trying to do both my day job and passion when I got home, something was still missing. I hadn't committed yet. On that day, I decided it was time to go All-In.

I quit my job at the consulting firm and never looked back. I walked out of that office feeling as though I had left prison and was now free. It was time to turn all my attention to becoming who I wanted to be. Not who society wanted me to be. Not who my parents, friends, bosses, and girlfriends wanted me to be. Who I wanted to be. I focused all my attention on the things that I wanted. The right things. The things that aren't based on what society tells me I should want. I put all my energy into my passion and living out my purpose of serving people.

Was I absolutely terrified? You bet. Did I have any idea how I was going to do it? Nope. Was I broke and not in a position to abruptly leave my job? Yep. But, that didn't matter. If I wanted to become the person I've always dreamed of becoming, I had to be bold. I had to take massive, determined action. It was the only way.

Now, I'm certainly not telling you to up and quit your job on the spot like I did. That was definitely not the smartest course of action. But, if you are unhappy with the life you're living there is only one person to blame – you. Believe me, I tried blaming everyone else and it doesn't work. You're responsible for your own happiness and you need to rely on yourself to do what makes you happy. If you are determined to change your life, you need to decide right here and now. It's time to take massive, determined action.

Action, by definition, is: "the fact or process of doing something, typically to achieve aim." So, ready...aim... fire! Now that I had found my purpose, escaped my past, and quit my job - it was time to build a plan. Though action and change begin to happen simultaneously, we must navigate a plan first. Before I could fully change my old ways and move on to finding my peace, I needed to take action and design a plan for what my life would look like. It would be my road map and guide to living the life I always wanted.

What Is Your Mission?

For this next step, I needed more help. Let me take this time to introduce you to two new friends of mine - Tony Robbins and Joe Duncan. Yes, I do wish both were my actual friends because, well, Tony is a different breed of human and any guy like Joe who gets up *Before 5 am* to start crushing their dreams is a person I want to know… but that's beside the point. Maybe one day I'll be lucky enough to call these dudes my friends, but for now, I'll just keep pretending they are because it makes me feel good. Plus, they are both the ideal guys to learn from.

Tony Robbins is a personal hero of mine and I couldn't do this next part of my quest without him. He understands the true meaning of life – sincere and selfless contribution. Tony inspired me to take control of my mental, emotional, physical, and financial destiny. After diving into *Awaken The Giant Within*, I became committed to becoming the best version of myself and increasing the quality of my life. He, along with my beautiful sister, saved me from one of the darkest places I have ever been – that makes it my duty to do the same for someone else. It was time for me to decide if I was going to keep drowning in my sorrows or get up and take some action toward my new life. So, I got started.

Joe Duncan, the Founder of *Before5AM, The Impact Billions Movement,* and creator of *The Blueprint,* changed my life forever. He is a remarkable leader, motivator, and life coach. Joe believes that we all have something beautiful and unique buried deep within us, and through his teachings provides ways of finding those hidden gems. He strives every day to ensure we are all taking the appropriate steps to living a lasting and meaningful life.

He developed *The Blueprint* for people like me who are struggling to find their place in the world and get motivated to living out their true passion. I dove into his Blueprint and began going through his full process. Joe taught me, among countless other things, that "you have to design it before you can build it and that means sitting down and thinking about what you want your life to be like and how you are going to make those outcomes and experiences a reality..." So, with his teachings and Tony's, that's exactly what I did.

By this point, I already had my lists of what I did not like about myself, what my new purpose was, and the lessons I had learned along the way - so determining what needed to be done was relatively straightforward. I began by writing out who I wanted to be, what I found to be my life's purpose/mission, and the qualities I hold to fulfill that mission. I call it my, "Mission Statement." Here it is:

Mission Statement:

"I believe my life's purpose is to change this world – one soul at a time. Steve Jobs said the people who are crazy enough to believe they can change this world are the ones who do.

"My mission on this quest of life is to serve and impact as many lives as I can through writing, communicating, and motivating people to find peace. I wish to live with integrity, impact lives and leave a lasting legacy on this world. I know, with certainty, I will do just that."

To Fulfill This Mission:

I have Empathy: I seek first to understand, and then be understood.

I Sacrifice: I devote my time, talents, and resources to my mission.

I Inspire: I have a background in Pain and a future in Peace. I've endured emptiness in my life, but pulled myself out of the trenches. This makes it my duty to help people do the same.

I am Impactful: I have a passion for people and understanding them on a deeper level. I'm not a surface friend. I'm much better at knowing everything there is to know and determining how I can help.

I am Persistent: I will not give up on my dreams and I will not settle. I have constructed a road map for my life and know, with certainty, what I will accomplish.

I am Present: I live with intention and follow through

These Roles Take Priority In Achieving My Mission:

Son/Brother: My family is the most important entity of my life. I am 'present' and always there for support, encouragement, and love.

Christian: I have a relationship, not a religion. I rely on God to guide me through the good and the bad, rejoicing in both.

Neighbor: I love my neighbor as myself and it is visible through my actions.

Writer/Speaker/Motivator: I am a catalyst for encouraging people to find success, happiness, and Peace in their lives.

Entrepreneur: I take risks, always believing in my abilities to win.

Scholar: I am a lifelong learner.

It was important for me to start with the why. We cannot find our peace and fulfillment until we understand why we want what we want. I want what I just shared with you because serving and helping people is the one thing on this planet that brings me the most fulfillment. I knew, with certainty, that this was going to be my life's work and why I was put here.

Develop A Road-Map

It was time for me to develop a plan for how on Earth I was going to achieve my purpose. So, I started small. Being goal oriented was not my strong suit. Sure, I was always ambitious and wanted to be great - but I lacked the fundamental ability to take action, plan, and then execute those plans. If procrastination and being unorganized had a son, it was me (no offense Mom and Dad, it surely wasn't your doing). But I changed my ways, and so can you.

I wrote out some immediate goals and life goals of what I wanted and why I wanted them so I could begin planning. It was challenging, and I had no idea where to start. But once I forced myself to start, it became a lot easier than I thought it would be. Here it is:

Goal	Why
100 days Sober	I want to see clarity. I want to know what it feels like to do 100 days completely sober.
Lose 50 pounds total and be healthy	I want to be healthy and have natural energy. I want to feel confident again.

Write a book about Finding Peace	I want to tell my story about addiction, bullying, depression and tragedy so I can help the world find peace with whatever pain they are struggling with. I believe I have a story to tell and can help at least one person. That is my goal.
Develop a Regimented Schedule	I want to get in a routine and stick to it. Days, months, years planned out and feel accomplished everyday
Clear $80,000 worth of debt	I want to be free from my debt so I can focus on helping people
Start a blog	I want to tell my story about addiction, bullying, depression, personal tragedy and what I want through so maybe it can help people
Write a screenplay	I want to tell the story of Luded and show people that striving for fame in a dark world will leave you lost and broken

Be a faithful husband and a loving father	I want to mimic my father and love my family unconditionally like he does. I want to be a truthful and honest man, like my father, and treat my family the way they deserve to be treated
Learn Real Estate	I want to learn real estate and use it as a platform to build my stability and raise a beautiful family in a nice home
Become a millionaire	I will become a millionaire because I never want to feel the insecurity & stress of not having money. The quicker I become a millionaire the more people I can help.
Pay off parent's debt	I want to be financially stable enough to give my working class parents what they have always deserved; freedom.

Impact millions of lives	I want to share my trials and lessons and try to help people. Knowing I served millions of people by helping them find peace would bring me the most fulfillment

Once I made this list and saw it written down on paper, an overwhelming amount of clarity struck me. Yeah, I had made some New Year's resolutions in my day to not do this and not do that - but nothing even close to this. And a majority of the time I never even followed through with those resolutions. I had never taken the time to think about what it was I actually wanted. It amazed me. How can someone live their life trying to be successful without even knowing what it is they want and why they want it?

Sure, I made it to my job on time (usually) every day, paid (some) of my bills and went to the gym once...a year (tragic I know). But I was walking around aimlessly without a plan in place to conquer what I wanted to. Did I know what I wanted to do with my life? Are you kidding? I didn't even know what I was doing tomorrow, let alone the rest of my life. The moment I wrote the goals down and I saw exactly what I wanted in my life, it became easy to start planning how I would get them. I mean if I could plan events and coordinate hundreds of drunk kids all over the city (Luded), I could sure as hell plan out what I was going to do with my life.

Goal Setting For Dummies

Goal setting is challenging. I won't sit here and say it isn't. I've read everything you can think of on goal setting and I still don't have it all figured out. But, I use the S.M.A.R.T. goal setting method and it works for me: Specific, Measurable, Attainable, Relevant, and Timely. Here's an example: Say you want to make $100,000 next year. Saying you want to make that amount of money is one thing but actually doing it is another. You need to break it down to make it realistic. So, $100,000/12 months = $8,333 per month. 8,333/30 days = 277. So, your goal should be written out like this:

Goal - Make $277 per day so I can make $100,000 next year

Make sense?

The next step in taking action was for me to break down my goals into categories and put a time frame on when I wanted to accomplish them. Here are the categories that I created based on my goal list: Daily Life, Finances, Fitness & Health, Writing, Serving People.

Breakdown Of Goals - 90 Day Action Plan

Daily Life

1. 30 days sober from this day on
2. Regimented Schedule implemented starting today (written out below)
3. Healthy and confident starting today
4. Happy and Motivated starting today
5. Truthful and genuine starting today

Regimented Schedule

Monday-Friday

6:00 a.m.	– Drink water, Make Bed, Watch Mission Videos, 6 Min Routine (SAVERS), Read 10 pages of a book, Write in Journal
7:00 a.m.-9:00 a.m.	– Gym, shower, breakfast
9:00 a.m.-12:00pm	– Read & Comment on an article, Finances, Write 200 Words, Book

12:00 p.m.-2:00 p.m.	– Lunch, Light Reading, Pod Cast
2:00-4:00 p.m.	– Learn something – Marketing, Public Speaking, Real Estate
4:00 p.m.-6:00 p.m.	– Write/work on book
6:00-8:00 p.m.	– Dinner + me time (NO PHONE)
8:00-9:30 p.m.	– Write, marketing, blog
9:30 p.m.-10:00 p.m.	– Evening Ritual, 3 things that went right, Drink water, read, prepare for tomorrow, sleep

Saturday

8:00-12:00 a.m.	– Wake up, breakfast, Gym, etc.
12:00-2:00 p.m.	– Write
2:00	– OPEN

Sunday

8:00-1:00 a.m	– Wake up, breakfast, run, church, etc.
1:00 p.m	– OPEN
8:00 p.m	– Review previous week, plan new week

Finances

1. Save $7,500 by March 1st
2. Pay off credit cards by April 1st

3. Pay off loans by December 1ˢᵗ
4. Completely Debt free by January 1ˢᵗ
5. Credit score over 700 by May 1ˢᵗ,

Fitness & Health

1. Strict diet with meal prep consistently
2. Gym at least 3 days per week
3. Weigh 200 lbs by March 1ˢᵗ
4. Regular doctor visits 3 times per year

Writing

1. Complete book by January 1ˢᵗ
2. Launch blog by January 1ˢᵗ
3. Begin Writing Screenplay by March 1ˢᵗ
4. 15 Content Pieces minimum posted on blog by March 1ˢᵗ
5. 5 Journal Entries per week

Serving People

1. Find at least one person to help everyday
2. Volunteer twice a month
3. Begin quest to impact millions of lives – now

Starting with a Daily Life category was the best move I could've made. It helped plan out my day and get me motivated early. Because I had spent years in nightlife and enjoy my beauty sleep, I've always been a bit of a night owl. Waking up earlier was quite a challenge for me at first. Though I haven't been able to fully jump on the Before5AM trend like my pal Joe, 6:00 a.m. was doable for me. I started with waking up 15 min earlier than I normally did and accomplished that for a week. Then the next week 30 min, and so on and so forth.

Like all things, it took time and patience. The trick was starting the night before. For instance, I lay out all of my clothes, down to my socks, the night before so I don't have to worry about what I'm wearing when I'm stumbling around my room at 'O Dark Thirty. You could always go a step further and do what the billionaire Mark Zuckerberg does - buy duplicates of the exact outfit and wear the same clothes over and over again to 'limit the time spent on making frivolous (whatever that means) decisions so you can concentrate on real work...' Well, Mark, not everyone created Facebook and has the confidence you do to wear the same thing every day - so, you go Glenn CoCo.

Anyway, like I was saying, 6:00 a.m. I could accomplish. I began each day with a 6-minute routine (SAVERS) in which I picked up from Hal Elrod who wrote, "The Miracle Morning." I adopted my own method to the routine which is a bit longer, but it's still based on the 'not so Shallow Hal' Elrod plan. Here it is:

Minute One: Silence

It's important not to start my day in a panic, rushing around trying to get it started. I did that for years and it resulted in the rest of my day being unorganized and stressful. So, a peaceful minute of silence before I set out to conquer the world always makes me feel relieved.

Minute Two: Affirmations

I went on Amazon and bought those little yellow Legal Notepads to write out my affirmations every morning. These are important. They are short, easy reminders of who you are and what you are capable of. I had no idea what affirmations were so I googled 'affirmations for dummies' and had my mind completely blown. These simple reminders help motivate me every single day.

Minute Three: Visualization

This was a tough one for me at first. I didn't know where to start and how to visualize who I wanted to be. So,

I created a photo album on my IPhone called "Vision Board" and threw in some pictures I found on Google of all the things I wanted in my life. Yes, I'll admit, I found some epic pictures of Tony Robbins speaking to hundreds of people and threw those in there. I also threw in some peace & motivating pictures, a range rover, a really nice house, and a picture of "The Rock" in terrific shape (no judgments).

Minute Four: Exercise

No. I will not sit here and tell you that this one is easy. I hate this one, but I do it anyway because it gives me more energy throughout my day. When I was younger, exercise was easy because I liked it. Now, I hate it because it's harder to lose weight. But with that said, it was only for a minute, so I stopped complaining and got it done. I do pushups, sit ups, or ride on my exercise bike (yes I have an exercise bike, don't tell anyone).

Minute Five: Reading

I read quite often now, so this one is also easy for me. However, I didn't always like reading especially first thing in the morning. I do daily devotions (yes, back to the God thing) because learning from Him as taught me how to love the life I live again. Might as well start my day off reading something inspiring, right?

Minute Six: Scribing

3 Things You Are Grateful For

3 Things You Are Committed To

A Few Words to Describe Your Current State

1 Joke To Calm The Storm

3 Goals To Live Out Your Purpose Today

There you have it, the 6-minute routine. Have you heard my construction joke yet? Never mind I'm working on it (Dad jokes are everything)… but once I worked on starting my day out with that quick routine, it changed my life. I went from sprinting around my room and hitting my shin on the corner of the bed trying to get ready in the morning to starting my day out on a peaceful note - ready to conquer the world.

Creating Small Wins

After that's finished, I write out 3-5 goals in which I would like to get done that day. It had to be extremely basic so I did not get discouraged if I fell short on one or two. It's a slippery slope. In the beginning, I would put tough tasks and overload myself. Once I did not complete one or two things it slowly turned into not completing any of them. I would get angry and crumple up the paper and throw it into the corner trash can yelling, "Kobe."

I think we all need to understand that failure is enviable. All success requires some sort of failure. So, to deal with failure in one arena, all you need to do is accomplish something in a different one. Call them small wins if you will.

I had to be realistic and write out things I knew, without a doubt, I could accomplish. Putting stuff like "3000 words written for my book" or "Lose 10lbs today" were unrealistic for me to achieve. So, I wrote things like "Help one person today" or "Write 200 crappy words for my book." These things were small wins that I could get done. And those small wins snowballed into me completing more things throughout the day.

Once I complete that, I write in my journal. This is important for me to do every single day because it's the one place where I'm always the most honest with myself. I write freely knowing that no one will ever read what is in there. It's helped a lot over the course of my Quest with healing my pain and understanding what this world has taught me. It was important for me to track my progress and reassures that I'm making the right moves.

After that, I move on to my finances. This is critical to me. For many years, I had zero idea what my financial situation looked like (I'll get into that later). But carving out a few minutes every morning to review my finances has drastically improved my situation. Right after that, I always tidy up around the house (something I never used to do at all) and then begin writing and planning my day. This part is ever changing now because my days are always different, but it's important to review my calendar and create a daily action plan for myself. I use the three goals for the day in which I already jotted down and do my best at timing out everything so I can stick to the schedule.

Once I got in a groove, I started creating a daily action plan for myself the night before so I could get going on it right away. My days are typically planned out by the hour so I can stay focused on getting everything I want to be done. It didn't happen overnight, but I got there.

If you have a day job, I'm sure the next eight hours of your life are already determined for you. I'm sure you do your best at hitting the gym and listening to some podcasts throughout the day to keep your brain fresh, but for the most part, your day job is a grind. I get it. Oh well. I don't care. When you get home from work, your day has just started. Remember, you're determined to accomplish the things you want, so you need to stay focused even when your day job ends.

Right when you get home every day, immediately put your phone on the charger in your room and don't go back to it for an hour. I still do this today. I believe technology consumes us all, and I was one of those people who checked my Facebook, Snap, and Instagram every four minutes. Talk about FOMO (fear of missing out for you non-millennials). That needed to stop. So every single day I spend at least one hour not looking at my phone. I did, and still do, all kinds of different things in this time - read, write, go to my pool, exercise, meditate, you name it. Anything to keep me away from technology for at least one hour. I always return after that hour feeling reenergized and happy.

The next hour and a half or so I spend making dinner and relaxing. It's important to unwind, get a good meal in your system, and not focus on work for a bit. I make it a point to do this every night. After that, it's back to the grind for me. For the next three hours, you will catch me learning real estate, writing or finishing up any tasks

I did not complete throughout the day. This time is vital because it's always my quiet time where I get the most done. When I'm finished with everything, I write out a short action plan for my next day, lay out my clothes, read, and then hit my bed feeling more accomplished than I did the day before. BOOM! I started cranking out my goals faster than Phelps swims the 100 meter.

Finances

"A budget is telling your money where to go instead of wondering where it went" *–John Maxwell*

Now that I had my goals mapped out and created a regimented schedule to stick to - it was time to shift my focus to finances. This step was one of the hardest steps in my entire Quest. My finances were an absolute mess. I had spent years of partying and neglecting my bank account completely because I was terrified of what I would find. I'm not kidding. I made it a point to pay as little attention as I possibly could to where my money was going and the amount of debt I was in.

I remember leaving $4 of credit left on one of my three already maxed out credit cards just so I could fill up my tank with it. I learned that as long as there is some credit left you can run it at the pump and it will allow you to fill your tank forcing you over your limit on the card. Yeah, it was that bad. Whatever it took for me to keep partying though, right?

I finally decided to create an action plan to get my finances in order and boy, did it suck - royally. I had to start somewhere so I did some research and found a few books to get me going. *"Rich Dad, Poor Dad"* by Robert T. Kiyosaki and *"The Total Money Makeover"* by Dave Ramsey are the two best beginner finance books I found - and trust me, I read several of them. There are a few others out there like, I will teach you to be Rich by Ramit Sethi, Personal Finance in your 20's for Dummies by Eric Tyson, and The Richest Man in Babylon by George S. Clason. I found these to be useful as well. But, for the most part, I stuck with the first two for my beginner books about finance.

The first thing I did was pull my credit report to see what the damage was. It was 548. Looking at that score and seeing all the items in collections brought me to tears. I'm not joking. I cried like a baby and hated myself. I was $80,000 in debt, behind on every single payment I was supposed to making, and completely and utterly disgusted with myself. But, instead of running like I used to, I took action and told myself I would never be this low again.

I created a budget based on the exact amount of money I had coming in per month (from writing and various online marketing ventures) with the amount of money I had going out. I found Mint to be the most helpful. It links with all my credit cards/bank accounts and breaks down all my spending categories for me. It's epic, and tragic at the same time. I found out quickly where all my money was going. Little did I know, I was spending almost $200 a month in just Ubers home from the bar. Who does that? I could buy groceries for three months with $200…or 400 tacos at Jack-in-the-box for that matter.

After I had created a fixed budget for myself, I knew how much money I could spend on paying my debt back. That would require me not to go out anymore, and live a very strict lifestyle. As *Dave Ramsey* puts it, "If you will live like no one else, later you can live like no one else." Simple enough, Dave.

For the next step, I created a spreadsheet and contacted every single debt collector on that report and negotiated a payment plan with each of them.

"Hi _____ my name is Ryan Jones, and I am calling because I spent countless years neglecting my finances and decided to be an adult and not do that anymore because finding out how much debt I was in royally sucked. So, I see I owe _____, and though I cannot make a payment today, I would like to speak to you about working out a payment plan that meets my budget. I can spend _____ per month paying you back, and that's all I can manage. What can you do for me, chief?

I spoke confidently knowing that I had a plan and they would work with me. Once creditors sense any weakness in your voice, they will pounce. So I didn't give them a reason to take advantage of me. I went in with a plan and was stern with what I could do, and they worked with me. At the end of the day, they just want to be paid, so I made them meet my demands. There you have it. I was on my way to financial freedom.

The spreadsheet started with the lowest debts I had. Dave calls this, "The Debt Snowball." There were a few outstanding utility bills that were less than $100, so I paid those off immediately by talking the creditor into settling for half what was owed. When I paid off that first balance and put a line through it on my list, I immediately became addicted.

I had a unique ability to obsess and become addicted to things, as I'm sure you gathered. So, I channeled that obsession into paying off debt, and my credit score jumped substantially along with my mental attitude. I could now see myself changing at a rapid pace and started feeling happy again. It was time to see what else I could do.

Health & Fitness

"Losing weight means you'll look good in clothes. Exercising means you'll look good naked." *Julia Stecher* (Fitness Model/Coach)

The next action plan was my health. Your health is everything, and if you let it go like I did you'll find yourself fat, single and sweating all the time. Gross, right ladies?

The first thing I changed was my diet. I was eating anything I could get my hands on. Because I lived in San Diego, California burritos with extra sour cream after a long night out were my weak spot. I cut those out immediately - along with booze, pizza, fast food, and anything else good... Okay, okay, there are tons of other good foods out there that are healthy for you but we can all agree those things are tough to pass up, yeah?

I cleaned up my act, went to Trader Joe's, and started meal prepping. The cool part about meal prepping and not eating out all of the time was that I saved a bunch of money in the process. I was under the assumption that eating healthy was more expensive, but Trader Joes is actually perfect for anyone on a tight budget. I came up with a new diet plan for myself and here it is:

Monday – Friday

Breakfast: Yogurt, granola, cliff bar, eggs, or oats w/ honey

Lunch: Chicken & Brussel sprouts; Ground Turkey & Quinoa; Chicken Salad

Dinner: Chicken & veggies, Squash Pasta, Steak & veggies, Carne on lettuce w/ balsamic, salmon and veggies

Weekends

One day the same as above

One Cheat Day: sushi, pizza (if you must), Greek food, Mexican (no sour cream), etc.

Doing a diet like that and sticking to it drastically changed my health. The next thing I did was find a buddy who was an avid gym goer and picked his brain. Because I was the true definition of "beginner" when it comes to anything fitness, I needed some guidance on how to live a healthy life.

That brings us to my next inspiring friend, Braun Wilburn (and yes, he's actually my friend). Braun is a Fitness & Health coach, model, hard 10, and all around gem of a human being. I'll let him take it away from here:

(Written by Braun Wilburn)

My Knowledge:

> *Weight lifting & anything relatively fitness related has played such an important, influential, and crucial role in my life for as long as I can remember! Being an athlete my entire life, fitness was really the only thing I ever found value in and truly loved. Nowadays, I lift once per day for about an hour and a half to two hours five times per week. I still find sanity and solitude in the gym. It truly is my place of peace and cant ever imagine a day without it. I even feel guilty not going on my "rest days"!*

> *I've experimented with all the latest and newest supplements on the market and after countless years of wasting money on products,*

112

experimenting with different workout styles, and overall taking the time to really understand what my own body responds best to - I came to the logical conclusion that I should not hide my knowledge and experience from those who want the help to change their lives. I truly get substantial amounts of joy and satisfaction helping people change their lives!

The Perfect Body

The fitness industry itself is a very unique industry unlike any other. Every person has a very different opinion on what methods work and do not work. This coordinates with the simple fact that every body reacts to methods differently. What works for me may not work for you, vice versa. That being said, it's often hard to develop guidelines and rules to the proper and efficient way of burning fat or building muscle or even maintaining current weight and body appearance. We are all precious little snowflakes; each one is unique and different in our own way.

Today, our society is plagued with the images of what the ideal "perfect body" looks like. The honest truth, put simply, is the perfect body is a body that you feel comfortable and confident in. The images that various companies promote for advertisements are in reality extremely unhealthy to try and maintain year round. On most occasions, the fitness models used in these advertisements prepare for these photo-shoots in the same ways that they prepare for their own physique competitions. These methods include: macro molecule manipulation such as carb cycling, cutting down their caloric intake to the bare minimum needed for survival, and proper reduction of water intake which provides a promotion of vascularity as well as the shredded / muscle striation appearance. Carrying that kind of body year around can have horrible repercussions on your health! Hormone imbalance, rapid weight fluctuation, organ damage, drastic mood swings, as well as mental and physical exhaustion are just a few that I can mention and most likely the most common.

Supplements

Supplements are plastered all over social media platforms as well as all over the Internet. "These supplements will give you insane muscle definition", "These pills will give you the 6-pack abs that you desire". The simple truth is supplementation can only help you in pursuit of the body that you desire but, they are not needed. Personally, I don't even drink protein shakes after my workouts... I maintain the body I have simply from the food I consume throughout the day. I do use pre-workout before my gym sessions but I prefer to mix it up with a cup of coffee on some days as well. You don't need supplements to get your ideal perfect body! It's all achievable without taking short cuts. Have a fairly clean diet, work hard in the gym, and promote a good calorie in vs. calories out mentality.

Diet

Dieting today has evolved to benefit everyone! Yes, I said everyone! The old ways of eating skinless chicken breast with rice and veggies is over. Most trainers today use the dieting system IIFYM (If It Fits Your Macros) which was developed by bodybuilders who grew tired of eating the same thing (what I listed above) 5-6 times per day for months at a time while preparing to step on stage for their competitions. With simple math, IIFYM helps you determine what your daily caloric intake should be (depending on your goal) as well as break down how much of each macromolecule (Carbs, Fats, & Proteins) you would need to hit your daily caloric goal.

Why is IIFYM important to you? The answer is simply that you can eat whatever you want! Yes, I said it, WHATEVER you want! If you want to start your day off with three delicious doughnuts then why not? All I will say back to you is IIFYM. However, it's not just a free for all diet strategy. For example, if you would like to start your day off with 3 doughnuts, you will most likely have to take into account that your meal at the end of your day will have to be relatively extremely low in fat considering you most likely used up all or almost all of your allowed fat intake per day. Everything is correlated and coordinated when it comes to you macro breakdown throughout the day. Its effective and efficient while also allowing you to still enjoy the foods you love. It is especially effective for trainers to use with their clients because diet is usually the most difficult part of the whole process for a client to grasp. It just makes a very complicated physiological system relatively easy for a beginner to understand.

Workout Routines

There are many efficient forms of workouts floating around out there depending on your goals of course. I've personally found that what works best of beginners is to always keep the body guessing. No, im not saying to go in the gym and lift every muscle group together. Im saying to switch up your exercises. When you perform the same exercises in the same pattern every time, your body will begin to plateau which results in being a complete waste of your time. Switch up the corresponding muscle groups as well.

Typically, you would lift Chest & Triceps together, Back & Biceps together, legs & shoulders individually. Some weeks, work each of theses muscles individually to shake things up. You can also switch those groups up where you feel is best. Sometimes ill work Biceps & Triceps together, or Chest & Biceps together, and isolate the remaining muscle groups to their own individual days. Increase your rep range and sets.

I personally start with my first at 15 reps at a manageable weight and deduct by 2 reps every set all the way down to 6 reps (15,12,10,8,6) while increasing my weight by 5-10 pounds every set. If you want to build muscle mass, lift heavier weight with lower rep ranges (6-8 Reps) and take a good amount of time to rest between sets. If you want to burn fat during your workouts, keep your intensity high by resting 30 seconds between sets. You can also super set for intensity purposes. This is where you work 2 antagonistic muscles in the same set. An example of this would be performing dumbbell bench press with a bent over dumbbell row. Bench press is a push exercise whereas the bent over row is a pull exercise.

If you would like to tone your muscles, stick to high reps and high sets and slow down the movement of your exercise and focus on your mind to muscle connection. Flex your muscle at the top of the exercise and release the movement slowly all the way down and repeat. If you are determined to burn off stubborn body fat, give HIIT cardio and workouts a try. Do this three times per week and your body will burn fat all week long even when not working out. HIIT stands for High Intensity Interval Training. It can be performed on a bike, treadmill, or my personal favorite the Stairmaster. Set the level of intensity on a level that is relatively easy to you and after 30 seconds increase it by two times your starting number and perform for 30 seconds. Once you finish that 30 seconds go back down to your original level and repeat.

Do this for 20 minutes (10 Intervals) and that's it. Do this after your weightlifting of course. You can find all kinds of HIIT workouts and cardio online!

Feel free to contact me directly if you have any questions in your pursuit to change your life. I'd be happy to help!

-Braun Wilburn
@itsbraunwilburn

See, I told you guys he was a gem. Braun keeps me motivated and I'm in the gym five days a week consistently. I went from being 254lbs and hating myself, to 200lbs and loving myself in 6 months. It was the change I needed to feel confident in myself that I was doing the right things. Taking action with my health helped in more ways than I ever imagined. It transcended me into a very positive mental state.

Become What You Are Committed To

The final step in taking Action was to create an "I'm Committed To" list in which I carry with me everywhere

I go. This is one of the most important things you can ever do to live a successful and purpose filled life.

I went to the store and bought 3x5 Notecards to write on. Yes, we are in a digital age but something about hand writing this step makes it more powerful. On one side, I split the card in two with a drawn line down the middle. On the left side, I write the date and under it my daily goals I wish to accomplish. On the right side, I write "100% Committed To" with a line under it. This is where I write out ALL the things I am 100% committed to so I can read them every single day. It's the fuel that keeps me burning inside.

Then, on the other side of the notecard, I write out a quote and a few words from my mission statement that inspire me to keep moving forward. I typically write, "We Become What We Are Committed To" on the top. Then, under it, "I believe my life's purpose is to change this world – one life at a time."

We need to form new ways of thinking if we ever want to progress. We cannot expect to do the same old things repeatedly and get different results. Laying a foundation for how you want to change your life is key to growth. We all need a road map to follow if we want to reach our intended destination. That road map is our lifeline to achieving an aim.

I had laid the foundation and was now well on my way to completely changing my life.

> *"The secret of change is to focus all of your energy, not on fighting the old, but on building the new."*
>
> **—Socrates**

Part Three – Action

1. Mission Statement
   1. Begin by writing who you want to be and what your life's mission is
   2. Start with why
   3. Card in pocket with Definiteness of Purpose
   4. Morning, mid-day, nightly vision and rehearsed purpose

2. Develop a Road Map
   1. Start small, don't get overwhelmed
   2. Write out some immediate goals and life goals
   3. Then write out why you want them

3. Break-down Goals into categories with a Time Frame
   1. Some categories to get you started: Daily Life, Finances, Fitness & Health, Career/Purpose, Serving People.
   2. Create a 90 day action Plan for completing these goals

4. Create a Regimented schedule
   1. Complete mapped out plan of everyday
   2. Start by waking up earlier and writing out a plan
   3. Morning time & 6 minute routine

4. Write out 5 goals you want to accomplish that day (create small wins)

5. Write in a journal

6. Use apps and set reminders for yourself to get things done

7. Spend at least one hour off the phone (meditating, reading, etc.)

5. Finances
   1. Create a budget
   2. Pull your credit report
   3. Make a budget
   4. Create a spreadsheet for debt (pay off lowest balance first)
   5. Live like no on else

6. Health
   1. "Losing weight means you'll look good in clothes. Exercising means you'll look good naked." *Julia Stecher* (Fitness Model/Coach)
   2. Diet plan
   3. Get a gym buddy

7. Become What You Are Committed To
   1. "I'm Committed To" list

2. 3x5 Notecard in pocket everyday

3. On side (goals + 100% committed to list)

4. Other side (quote + mission statement)

If you'd like to begin your own Peace Quest, you can find the Ebook with worksheets and a detailed plan to Taking Action on the website <u>www.ThePeaceQuest.com</u>

CHANGE YOUR AUTOPILOT – STEP 4

"The definition of insanity is doing the same thing over and over again, but expecting different results. We cannot solve our problems with the same thinking we used when we created them."

—Albert Einstein

You will not find Peace until you learn how to change your autopilot.

Have you heard my airplane joke? Never mind – it's over your head (Dad Jokes Matter).

On January 15th 2009, US Airways Flight 1549 was scheduled for departure from LaGuardia Airport in New York. As passengers settled into their seats and listened to the same boring safety presentation, the two pilots began their typical routine of prepping the plane for takeoff. Once they received clearance from control, they approached the runway, entered any last minute weight changes, assessed any wind shifts, adjusted speeds, set the flaps and then completed the takeoff checklist (like they had done a million times). After the throttles were turned up, the power was set, and one final clearance... the pilot began takeoff.

In the climb-out after takeoff, the plane struck a flock of geese and lost all engine power. Pretty much the worst possible luck, ever. Unable to reach any airport and running out of options as they descended, the pilot (Chesley Sullenberger) opted to 'glide' the plane into the Hudson River – saving all 155 souls on board. The event became known as the "Miracle on the Hudson."

Sometimes, we are thrusted into circumstances that seem beyond our control. We have a routine – our own specific way of doing things. Call it our personal autopilot if you will. This autopilot, good or bad, is what works for us. We're accustomed to it and don't really see a need to alter it.

Then, a flock of geese swarms in and blows out the engine - propelling us into a downward spiral. Gives me goosebumps just thinking about it (see what I did there?). In a moment of decision, we're forced to change our autopilot, alter the course and hope we land safely in a river somewhere.

Change, by definition is: "the act or instance of making or becoming different." We all need to change and become different if we want to grow. I could find my purpose, escape my past, and take all the action I wanted - but I would not get to peace until I changed my habits and autopilot.

Humble Yourself

The first step in changing myself was understanding there were things that needed to be changed. I had to tell myself I was ready to alter the course, change my habits and begin living the life I always wanted. It was Rick Warren who taught me that "we become what we are committed to." I committed to creating a new autopilot, along with a new way of thinking, so I could fully change and be the person I wanted to be.

I was terrified at first and had no idea where to begin. But, I just told myself to keep moving forward. Martin Luther King Jr. said, "If you can't fly, then run, if you can't run, then walk, if you can't walk, then crawl, but whatever you do, you have to keep moving forward." So, I kept pushing moved forward.

Brad had taught me a lot on my Quest to finding Peace, and he said something to me that I will remember for the rest of my life:

> "If you want to drastically change your life, you have to make drastic changes in your life. Change is a process, not just an action. It is the acknowledgement and understanding of wrongdoing, planning of the new course of action, implementing that new decision and monitoring the progress of your life after. Change can happen instantaneously or over time, depending on what you choose to do." -Brad Gardner

That pretty much summed it up for me. I did a lot of thinking in this time and started asking real questions to myself. What if it actually could happen? What if my mentality shifted? I began to think all the possibilities of my hopes and dreams could become a reality based on the attitude that what I wanted in life would happen if I was willing to change.

There is a difference between wishing to be successful and knowing you are going to be. Everyone who walks this earth wishes to be successful, but few know they are going to be. People who wish are constantly looking for the next great idea to come their way that will make them successful. People who know construct a plan and create opportunities for themselves because they want to change who they are and the world we live in.

Easier said than done though. In all reality, we shape our perspective around the path we walk and people we interact with. Our vision is skewed because we want to please and conform to the norm. We abide by the rules set by the individuals before us because it is the only truth we think we know. So, the only question worth asking is, how do we change it?

Luckily, I had already done most of the work - so this portion of the Peace Quest was a bit easier than the rest. I had already acknowledged my wrongdoing and planned a new course of action, so it was time to implement that plan.

I decided I wanted to write a book about finding peace and begin my journey to impacting millions of lives. As I was stumbling around trying to find my place in this world, I kept coming to the understanding that I was called to serve. I enjoy people. I like helping others achieve a goal and seeing people happy doing what they love.

So, I set out on the path to doing just that. It had been a rough road for me the past few years, but I learned that no matter what I am going through, no matter what pain I am feeling, no matter what struggles are present in my journey - there will always be someone out there who has more pain than I have. There is still someone struggling more than I am. There is still someone out there who could use my help in getting them through the day. That is the only thing that keeps me going. I can't quit on these people. They are holding on, and maybe I can help them in some way. I didn't know exactly how yet, but I did know I was going to try. I had begun to change.

Drop The Dead Weight – The Power Of No

I made a full commitment to myself to change for the good. The next step in changing was to cut the dead weight. I had done a lot of this already in Escaping my past, but I still had people and things in my life holding me back from being who I wanted to be. That ended right there. I needed to weave out the wrong people in my life.

Og Mandino said it best, "I will persist until I succeed. I was not delivered into this world into defeat, nor does failure course my veins. I am not a sheep waiting to be prodded by my shepherd. I am a lion, and I refuse to talk, walk, and to sleep with the sheep." Furthermore, I believe the old saying goes, "You spend too much time worrying what other people think of you…A lion doesn't concern himself with the opinion of a sheep." Though I absolutely DO NOT believe we should ever view the world as if we're better than anyone else - what I took from these quotes is that I could no longer allow the opinions of others to alter the pursuit of my dreams.

I started by making a list of five people who I spent the most time with. I wrote out a few character traits to describe them and why I felt they should be in my life for the future. I wasn't overly critical or overly nice. I was honest. The goal was to ensure these people were bettering my life and encouraging me to grow. It was Jim Rohn (motivational speaker) who said, "you're the average of the five people you spend the most time with." So, I needed to ensure they are the right people.

I made it my mission not to be better than others, but just to try and be better than I used to be. I read over the list and confirmed these people were bettering my future. If they are not, I learned the Power of "NO." I was certainly not rude to these people, nor did I inform them that they were 'no longer my friend' (because that would be tacky, and weird). I just started preoccupying myself with things to do so I could prepare a, "No, sorry I can't tonight, bro…" when they would call to hang out.

Once I separated from the people who were holding me back from accomplishing my goals, my entire life opened up. I learned the word "No" so I could finally do what makes me happy. And boy was this a tough one.

"Omnia?" the text read from Brian (my old boss). It was Friday night and Brian, along with a few others, were trying to get me out to the club…again. It was the standard deal. Grind all week and then buy a floor table at the best club in the city with whatever girls we could wrangle in. Against all odds, I replied with, "Not tonight my dude, I have dinner plans. Thanks though. Crush it for me." I didn't have dinner plans. In fact, I had no plans at all. Instead, I stayed in and wrote a book.

If I'm being completely honest, I had never felt that alone before. I realized that I was now walking the road by myself and it was one of the hardest things I have ever done. I didn't have the slightest clue what I was going to do or how this was all going to work out - but I did know being in that world of partying would not lead me any closer to happiness.

So, all I could do was try to be better every single day, and learn to say no to the people holding me back. I had begun climbing, and I would do it alone if I had to. Whatever it took to find my happiness and be successful, I would do. I would not quit. I would not give in. I would not let a girl, boss, bad friend or anyone else, win. I'm a fighter and a believer. A dreamer and achiever. It was time to separate myself and go after what I wanted. I was Three Feet from Gold.

National Peace Day (Yes, It's A Thing)

When I experienced my rock bottom, I decided it was time for me to change and be sober. Now, I've gone back and forth a hundred times with whether or not I should encourage people to do the same (if you're a drinker), and I finally decided that it's not up to me. That one is up to you. Being sober changed my life completely, but that doesn't mean it will do the same for you.

It was a goal I wanted to accomplish for me because it was the root of all my problems. Some people can have a glass of wine or two and call it a night. I would have a bottle and then go out to the club. Balance and knowing when to quit were not my strong suit (by any means). So, I needed to change.

I knew cold turkey was out of the question because going from the amount I was drinking to quitting overnight for the rest of my life was just not realistic. When deciding I wanted to change the things about myself in which I was unhappy with, it was important to make it realistic. I had to be certain that I could actually accomplish it. I made a goal for 30 days completely sober. It was nearly impossible, but I did it. And let me tell you why it was the coolest thing I ever did.

As fate would have it, when I sat down and counted out the days to 30 and wrote on the calendar "30 Days Sober" - in the right corner of that little box read "National Peace Day." I'm not joking. This really did happen, and it still gives me chills to this day. Talk about the universe aligning and giving me some clarity. It was a defining moment in my Peace Quest. It was the first time I had changed and conquered a goal that I set out to accomplish.

If I ever become stable enough to drink on occasion again, I made a promise to myself to always do 30 days out of the year, three times in that year, completely sober. If you're not one of those math geniuses out there, yes that means 90 days total completely dry broken down into 30 day periods. If there is a wedding or celebration in which I feel comfortable enough to not slip back into my old ways, then, sure, I may indulge a bit. But, I decided that immediately following that drink I would do 30 days without a drop. I believe 30 day periods give us the clarity we need at the end to continue living a happy life.

It gave me a level head, and it felt good to say no to people. People would try to get me to go out on weekends all the time. It was hard to say no, but I had committed to changing playmates and playgrounds leaving my old life behind me. Soon enough, they stopped asking.

Saying no to people who held me back is one of the toughest lessons I ever learned. But I had to do it. I surrounded myself with only people I knew would encourage me to grow. The list was small, but they were more than enough to help get me through. I won't bore you guys with my list here, but I will take this time to thank those people who stayed in my life and helped me grow (you know who you are because you had to listen to my sob story every time you called…you're welcome, I mean, thank you?).

Implement The Plan

In sticking with the airplane analogy, the aviation industry follows a strict principal known as the 60-to-1 Rule. The rule states that if a pilot is one-degree off course, he or she will miss their target landing spot by 92 feet for every mile (which equates to 1 mile off for every 60 miles they travel).

Meaning even the slightest degree off course could be the mistake that costs the pilot, and many others, their life.

The exact same logic applies for your road-map to success. After you develop the plan, you need to be intentional and follow it precisely.

After I had learned how to say no, I began implementing the plan and foundation I laid out for myself. I had my regimented schedule and roadmap to success - all I had to do now was follow it. I couldn't make all of the changes at once though. I tried, and became discouraged and ended up quitting on some of them. Small wins every day was the key.

Like I told you, when I planned out my day, in the beginning, I wrote out tasks in which I knew I could accomplish. It was simple things like, "Take out the Trash," "Call Mom and tell her you love her (because why not)," "Write 200 words" …It didn't matter how small the task was, just as long as I completed something I wrote down. There's no better feeling than crossing off and putting a checkmark next to things I got done. It helped me grow. And over time, those tasks became larger and larger, and I started seeing drastic improvements in my life.

I am a competitive person by nature, so I took this opportunity to compete with myself and try to accomplish more and more every week. I put tasks on a whiteboard in my room, challenging myself to do more than I did the week before. I made sure to stick to the plan I created, focused on improving myself, and was that much closer to finding Peace.

I stopped worrying about what other people were doing and how they were living their lives. It wasn't fair for me to judge them or think negatively about them. I could only be responsible for changing my own path. I needed to let others walk theirs. I witnessed a perfect example of why focusing on my path was vital to success from the *Rio 2016 Summer Olympics.*

Athletes, in their competitive nature, always strive to be the best. The elite, however, have already mentally grasped that they are the best and no one can stand in between them and their next victory. *Michael Phelps* of the United States is among these elite, and Chad le Clos of South Africa is the athlete in that famous photo we all saw of him looking to his left and watching Phelps pass him. If you don't remember the photo, *Google* "Phelps passes Chad le Clos" and see it for yourself (you're welcome).

Well, Mr. Clos, stay in your lane because Michael Phelps is the greatest Olympian in history and he is "too busy winning…" to focus on you. The significance of the image, taken in Rio from the Men's 200m Butterfly on Day 4 of the 2016 Olympic Games, is that in the weeks and hours leading up to this race Clos had shifted all of his attention to intimidating Phelps in any way he could.

Boasting to the press about his previous victories, dancing and parading around in the warm-up room, and staring down Phelps just minutes before the race. His sole motivation was on beating Phelps - not on preparing and winning the race for his own success. What he didn't realize at the time was that there is no 'getting inside Phelps' head.' Phelps' is the type of athlete who has spent years mentally preparing himself to 'lock-in' and set his mind on one particular goal: winning. He didn't need to respond. He didn't need to feed into the taunting.

In fact, I'd be willing to argue that he wasn't thinking of Clos at all. He had his sights set on standing up on that podium and looking at the American Flag raised higher than any other. Once that vision was made up in his mind and replayed over and over again, nothing else mattered. Clos didn't stand a chance.

It's fair to say that Rapper/Entertainer 50 cent said it best, "Winners focus on winning, losers focus on winners..." If I, and Clos for that matter, focused on staying in my own lane, things would undoubtedly work out differently, and I would find success. Plus, I heard when you're in your own lane, there is far less traffic (see what I did there).

So Much Room For Activities

That brings us to the next step in change. If I wanted to change, I had to start doing activities that were different than what I did before. Now that I wasn't drinking, I had to find things to occupy myself. Not only that, I needed to do new things so I could break my old habits. I started playing basketball, Frisbee golf, fishing, went on hikes, visited museums, and even tried yoga. I'm not kidding. My fat, lazy, inflexible-self turned off Netflix, got off the couch, and went to yoga. No, I didn't do it myself (because how the heck could I); I had some help.

Let me take this time to present you with my next inspiring friend on the list (there are a few in case you didn't notice). Ladies and gentleman, I am pleased to introduce you to Nicole Freeman. Nicole is a different breed of human altogether. Her independent, happy self is one of the kindest, loving, and inspiring people I have ever met. She loves this place we call Earth and finds her happiness all around her in the simple pleasures life has to offer. She is one of my closest friends and helped me a great deal in my Quest to finding peace.

Here's what she had to say on the topic of change… "Change. I know most people hate it, but I think constant change is healthy. Growth doesn't come from a place of comfort. My yoga instructor, Meredith, says yoga is helping us shed our layers…so constant change in who we are allows us to become better versions of ourselves." And right she is.

Nicole pulled me out of my place of comfort and encouraged me to grow. Though I do not see myself diving in full throttle and throwing on neon yoga pants in the near future - yoga is something everyone should try. It helped calm me down and inspires millions of people all over the world every single day. And if you're a single dude, it's like 90% woman there, so that was a huge bonus (just don't be weird about it).

Fishing and camping with my Dad and brother became a new norm for me as well. Even in the loneliness of the wilderness, a calming peace from the running stream took me away from the city noise and those attempting to alter my happiness. That running stream and the fish beneath didn't care if I was rich or poor, the kind of car I drove, or what my past entailed. Trout didn't ask questions or judge the things that I had done. They didn't care if I was wearing an expensive suit or a brown fishing vest with a fish hook hat to block the sun. They challenged me to be better while also calming the storm within. I learned that there was no wifi deep in the woods but that I would find a better connection. It taught me to slow down and enjoy my time spent with the people I love. I found peace in that wilderness, understanding that if a small creek could make its way through a Grand Canyon, I could make my way through life, too. (Maybe I should've been a poet).

Whatever activity I decided to do, I made it something different than anything I had ever done before. This was the time in my life where I got to try new things and develop new passions, and it didn't matter how old I was either. I think we can all learn to do new things and develop new passions whether we're 5 or 105, (though I do not recommend climbing Everest if you're 105).

People Helpin' People

The next step to change was find ways to help people. Up to this point, I was so consumed with bettering my own life and finding success that I had almost forgotten the central reason as to why we are all here. We are all called to serve. I don't care what God you believe in or if you believe in a higher being or not - we all will not find fulfillment until we have made some difference in this world.

We all need to feel useful as if our time spent here mattered. So, I was glad to see the purpose I found in the very first step of my Peace Quest had something that involved helping at least one person. Even if you think your job and life's work has nothing to do with serving people, I guarantee it does. If we didn't have garbage men, our trash would pile up in front of the door and we would never be able to escape the stench. So, if you're a garbage man, God Bless You.

Everything we do serves a higher purpose, and that's the way I needed to view the world. I started telling myself that the daily things I was doing were moving me towards something bigger than myself. That made it very clear and easy to catch when I was doing something that wasn't serving a higher purpose. And that is how I learned to change and grow.

We will dive deeper into helping people in the final step of your Peace Quest (Empathy), but for now start viewing the world as naturally good and try to find someone you can help.

Chop Wood

"Kenny, how the hell are you chief," I asked as I did my monthly check-in with my older cousin. "Doing alright, sh*t head, what's new? How are you holdin' up?" Though he may seem insensitive with the name calling, Kenny is the older brother I never had and someone I've looked up to since I was young. He's had a very successful career in commercial real estate after graduating from USC and has given me life advice most of my own life. I've called on him for many favors, and he has guided me along in times I had no one else to turn to.

"Oh, you know. Besides being tragically depressed while searching for direction on how I'm going to change this hopeless world…I'm fine. Thanks for asking. I have a question for you." Laughing, he responded with, "Of course you do. What's up?"

"Well, as you know, I've been doing some soul searching and trying to find ways to better my life. How do you stay consistent and not let daily struggles get you down?" Without missing a beat, he responded with, "Chop wood. It's as easy and hard as that."

The final step I needed to take in changing myself was to learn how to chop wood. No, Kenny wasn't talking about going in my backyard and hacking down a tree, only to have it come timbering down on my house creating more problems in my life. What he meant was to wake up every single day with an ax, ready to go to work. To make it in this world, I had to be willing to work harder than everyone else and prepare for the unexpected. If I planned, focused all of my energy on the right things, and then woke up in the morning ready to chop wood, I would find success. Then, and only then, I would begin to find my peace.

Change can happen instantaneously or over time, but we must always remember to hold our head up and keep moving forward. A turtle may move slowly, but that is why it has the toughest shell. If we're strong enough to ask the Universe for the right things, follow the foundation we've laid out, and wake up every day ready to chop wood - we'll find success.

As the man himself Mahatma Gandhi put it, "Be the change you want to see in the world." And it was almost time for me to go on and be that change. Now that I understood my purpose, escaped my past, put together an action plan, and laid the foundation to change - it was time to move on to the final step in my quest, Empathy.

Part Four - Change

1. Humble yourself
   1. Understand some things need to be changed

2. Drop the dead weight
   1. Weave out the wrong people in your life
   2. Learn the Power of "No."
   3. Fave-five list

3. Implement the plan
   1. follow it, precisely
   2. Focus on yourself, not others

4. So Much Room for Activities
   1. Find new, positive activities to occupy yourself
   2. take a leap of faith and do something outside of the box

5. People Helpin' People
   1. View the world as naturally good
   2. Find a way to serve it

6. Chop Wood
   1. Wake up every single day with an ax ready to go to work

If you'd like to begin your own Peace Quest, you can find the Ebook with worksheets and a detailed plan for Changing Your Autopilot on the website www.ThePeaceQuest.com

EMPATHY – STEP 5

"Only those who have learned the power of sincere and selfless contribution experience life's deepest joy: true fulfillment."
—Tony Robbins

You will not be at Peace until you have Empathy.

Loneliness, by definition (don't worry, I'll get to empathy), is: "the quality of being unfrequented and remote; isolation." For me, it's the word at the end that says it all. When you get to a point in your life when you don't have anywhere else to turn, that's called loneliness or complete isolation.

It haunts us all. In some way or another, we try everything to avoid it. We tell people what they want to hear. We do what they want us to do. We sacrifice our own happiness to ensure they are happy. We put ourselves down to make the ones around us feel at ease with themselves. We do it all only to isolate ourselves into complete loneliness. I received my first taste of it at a young age, and boy did it royally suck.

Does O'Doyle Rule?

We moved from our beautiful home in Rancho Cucamonga to Southern Illinois when I was a freshman in high school. For those of you who do not fully understand what that means to a young teen just starting puberty, let me paint a picture for you. There were 3,000 kids in my high school in Southern California, and there were less than 3,000 people in the entire town we moved to in Southern Illinois. You could say we stuck out like a sore thumb.

I showed up the first day of school wearing a red 'Quicksilver' sweater in which made me another face in the crowd when we lived in Rancho. In Benton Illinois, things were quite different. When I arrived, there were six kids huddled around a pick-up truck wearing overalls gripping onto the horns of a newly slaughtered deer from earlier that morning. I was far from home.

Not to say we were wealthy by any means, but we were from Southern California moving into a town where people thought everyone from California was straight from Beverly Hills, 90210 and the Real World. If you don't know what those shows are then, you apparently didn't live through the 90's. For you infants, it would be like "Keeping up with the Kardashians" or "The O.C." Anyway, I had zero friends from the start. And not only that, I was severely bullied.

My Mother, the saint, always told me 'hate' is a strong word and to never use it. Well, sorry, again, Mother- I hate bullies. In the small town we lived in, sports were everything because there wasn't much else to do. The town's pride and joy athlete saw me as someone who could threaten the legacy he built. So, his only move was to break me down entirely.

"Jones, I thought Cali kids were supposed to be 'California Dream Boats'…with your teeth looking like that and how you dress, you're more like a 'California Wrecked Boat," He clowned on the bus ride to our first game. Seeing the rest of the team staring and laughing, I jokingly deflected with, "Yeah, I guess I could use some new teeth…do you have any extra you could spare, chief." He, not amused, degradingly fired back with, "You need a lot more than new teeth, fag…keep your mouth shut so we don't have to look at it." Then, being the "cool kid" he was, followed by throwing all my gear out the window of the bus. Yeah, real cool he was. It was devastating and the hardest thing I had ever been through up to that point. The worst part was, there was absolutely nothing I could do. I was alone and ratting on him would only lead to everyone else hating me more. So, it continued.

I was put in trash cans, spit on, and an outcast from the day I set foot in that God-awful town. I didn't know how to tell my parents, or anyone for that matter, so the only thing I could do was bury it within and pray it would end soon.

I pretended to be sick at times to avoid going to school. It was like those scenes in Billy Madison where he fakes sickness by lying in bed with a heated thermometer to avoid facing O'Doyle. Then the maid, Juanita, would force him to go and face his fears.

> O'Doyle: Mortal Kombat for the Sega Genesis is the best game ever made.

> Billy Madison: I disagree. It's a very good game, but I think Donkey Kong is better.

> O'Doyle: Donkey Kong sucks!

> Billy Madison: Wanna know somethin'? You suck!

Then he would pour milk over Billy's head and chant, "O'Doyle Rules! O'Doyle Rules! Yeah, thanks a lot, O'doyle. It was nice to meet you…" It was just as awful for me as it was for Billy…and any other kid who has been bullied. We lasted six months and dipped out of there quicker than Usain Bolt runs the 100 meter.

I was happy to go, but that bullying, loneliness and overwhelming sadness stuck with me for years to come. Anyone who has suffered from bullying knows that it's the most traumatic experience a young person can go through. It usually occurs (but certainly not always) at a fragile time in your life as you are not quite sure who you are yet. You struggle every day trying to find your place with whoever you can; only to be tormented and belittled by the kids who are admired by everyone. It's a very lonely feeling and anyone who has felt that pain probably doesn't have the courage to tell you.

People will always find ways to discourage us from being who we want to be. Though it took me many years to learn this, we cannot allow them to. We're all beautiful in our own way; even if we have not found that beauty in ourselves yet.

As much as I wanted to fight back and tell O'doyle (bullies) to kick rocks - I didn't. Over time, I learned how to soften my heart and understand that maybe the kids who bullied me had their own struggles.

Though it affected me later, I developed a unique ability to hide my pain and continue living my life. I understood from a young age that everyone is hurting. Some people feel the urge to inflict that pain on others through bullying and putting people down. I made a decision to do my best at loving people and accepting them for who they were. I couldn't control bullies, so the only thing I could do was bury that pain deep within and do my best at seeing the good in people.

Attempting at being like O'doyle and putting others down surely doesn't rule...as I'm sure you witnessed the result in that scenario if you saw the movie.

Yep, you guessed it... Empathy, by definition, is: "the ability to understand and share the feelings of another." It is the full capability of you to be able to put yourself in someone else's shoes and view things from their perspective. It is understanding the feelings of what that person is going through and trying to find ways in which you can help them.

We're all each other's keepers, and need to find ways in which we can be there for people in times of need. The moment you discover you are not the only person walking this Earth who needs help and maybe you have the ability to help them, everything changes.

Life, A Precious Gift

They say April showers bring May flowers - but whoever 'they' are never expressed to us what those showers would consist of. On Friday, April 18th, 2008, just weeks before my High School graduation, showers of ash presented a gloomy May scarce of any flowers.

"Jones, I need you to come here a minute..." were the burning words Ted Persell, my varsity baseball coach, shouted from across the diamond. Those words would impact my immediate future - resulting in that urgent 'minute' he requested to feel like an eternity. Tired and winded from running sprints (running was not my strong suit), I jogged across that perfectly trimmed diamond only to find a look of desperation on his face.

It's remarkable how one interaction with another human can have a profound effect on the rest of our lives. Though I'm not entirely sure he was prepared to do so, the next words he spoke changed my life forever. I remember him looking me dead in the eyes with a new, almost rare compassion and whispered, "Your house is on fire, you need to get home as quickly as you can..."

He went on speaking, but I couldn't make out the words. It was as if my entire world paused after he said those first words to me. It was a surreal feeling. There I was, just minutes before, running sprints solely absorbed by my own exhaustion - only to be emotionally and physically weakened by the thought of what the events ensuing would mean for my family and me.

I arrived at my house, barefoot, and was tackled by a firefighter after running onto my lawn attempting to race inside our burning home and pull out any pictures or prized possessions I could. I was the first person from my immediate family on the scene, and I remember laying on my front lawn watching it burn feeling the most helpless I had ever felt.

My mother, who was at my brother and sister's school helping in the classroom, was my first phone call. The silence on the other end of the phone as I relayed to her the events that were currently burning our life apart is something I will never forget.

She always had a unique way of comforting us children, reminding us to love one another and not to be afraid because God has a plan. That moment was the very first time my mother was silent as if her world had been shattered. She arrived, with my brother and sister, shortly after that. I'll never forget her face as she looked up at the home, and life, her and my father had provided for us still up in flames.

From watching firefighters throw our prized possessions into a large dumpster, to seeing my mother drop to her knees in disbelief as she cried out to my Father hundreds of miles away, and then hearing the sobbing of my brother and sister - you could say it was the hardest, most emotional day of my life. Because my father worked hours away, he wasn't on scene to answer pressing questions from fire captains, police officers, insurance salespeople, and anyone else claiming they were there to help. So, that left me to be the man in charge.

It's still a blur to this day, but at that moment I was forced to grow up a lot faster than I intended. All I wanted to do was hold onto my family and sulk with them until my Dad arrived. But, answering questions I had no idea how to answer, from people who I had never even met, was what I found myself doing instead. To this day, I couldn't tell you if I said the right things or not to those people, but I guess that part doesn't matter. I was a senior in High School at the time, what did I know anyway? Or at least I'm sure that's what they thought. The only thing I can tell you is that this day was one of the hardest experiences of my life.

Though the fire was unable to bring our entire foundation to the ground, the smoke on the inside would prove to be enough to cloud our world from that day forward. As my loving sister would say, "the clues of our home facing deterioration internally could not be seen by a jogger or dog walker casually passing by... the gate, outlining the perimeter of our home, only gave away that something wasn't right; but the darkened glass windows shown a mere glimpse that something was broken and burned from a heat that damaged the soul of our home..."

Such is true about people too. Life seems all but normal on the outside, but little do they know an internal deterioration is burning us apart, piece by piece. We call out for help, only to be told to wait it out - the flames will soon stop burning. In turn, we build gates around our homes and hearts for fear of people entering and discovering our internally broken souls. 'The darkened windows are the only way to know, that looking into someone's eyes can reveal the unknown.'

The Fire marks the day that sent me on the path of total destruction. I became angry at God for putting my family, especially my mother, through something that was completely out of our control. In all reality though, and I didn't understand this until much later, the Fire marks the day when my family and I became closer than we'd ever been. I know, now, that possessions and material objects can vanish at any moment, but the ones you love are always with you.

Yes, I felt helpless, yet I am remarkably blessed that I still have the people in my life who I cherish the most. This day is a constant reminder to never be a surface friend to anyone who comes in my life. I now make it my mission to know people on a much deeper level because you never know when that person will vanish from your world – leaving you lost, broken, and wishing you had said more.

We were forced to live in a hotel for a while, and no it wasn't easy (by any means), but we did it together. We depended on each other and valued the fact that yes we lost our home and possessions, but we still had each other.

We all endure tragedy and hard days, but if you surround yourself with loving, caring people, you can overcome anything that life throws at you. Life is a precious gift given to us with the hope that we will love all the people and blessings it has to offer.

A Simple Gesture

This story I'm going to share with you is one of the most compelling stories I have ever read. It brought me to tears when I read it because I know what it feels like to not want to be alive anymore. It showed me the true meaning of empathy and how we should always treat others with love and compassion because we don't know what battle that person is fighting in their own life:

A Simple Gesture

Mark was walking home from school one day when he noticed the boy ahead of him had tripped and dropped all of the books he was carrying, along with two sweaters, a baseball bat, a glove and a small tape recorder. Mark knelt down and helped the boy pick up the scattered articles. Since they were going the same way, he helped to carry part of the burden. As they walked Mark discovered the boy's name was Bill, that he loved video games, baseball and history, and that he was having lots of trouble with his other subjects and that he had just broken up with his girlfriend.

They arrived at Bill's home first and Mark was invited in for a Coke and to watch some television. The afternoon passed pleasantly with a few laughs and some shared small talk, then Mark went home. They continued to see each other around school, had lunch together once or twice, then both graduated from junior high school. They ended up in the same high school where they had brief contacts over the years. Finally the long awaited senior year came and three weeks before graduation, Bill asked Mark if they could talk.

Bill reminded him of the day years ago when they had first met. "Did you ever wonder why I was carrying so many things home that day?" asked Bill. "You see, I cleaned out my locker because I didn't want to leave a mess for anyone else. I had stored away some of my mothers sleeping pills and I was going home to commit suicide. But after we spent some time together talking and laughing, I realized that if I had killed myself, I would have missed that time and so many others that might follow. So you see, Mark, when you picked up those books that day, you did a lot more, you saved my life."

Written by John W. Schlatter

Everyone we meet is fighting a battle in which we know absolutely nothing about. That inspiring story altered the way I view the world and how I choose to interact with people. I no longer allow someone to walk by me without acknowledging them with a simple smile or hello. A smile can be the reason that person decides to keep on living. There are people all around us with pain we fail to see every day. One 'hello' can change your life, or another's, and you won't know that until you befriend them.

Being bullied and attempted suicide are topics that I know all too well. For me, it was my sister who saved my life. She believed in me when I didn't believe in myself, and she is the reason I am here today. So, I'll let her tell you what it means to be empathetic.

Let Me Take A Selfie?

My 'Saint in Training' sister, Jessica (or as I like to call her 'Blessica'), is the most loving, caring and empathetic

160

person I know. So, for this last step in my Quest, I needed her to refresh my memory on the topic of Empathy.

Here's what she had to say:

"Empathy is perhaps one of the greatest gifts we can give to someone. Throughout this journey we find ourselves taking in discovering ourselves, one thing I know for certain is that to really come alive is to live outside of yourself.

Faith and love as a whole aren't circumstantial or a bases of feeling, but rather a state of being - a direct reflection of where our hearts are rooted and if peace is woven inside of that most sacred gift. However, empathy is distinctly different. It is a river from the soul and a place to dwell in. It is an act we constantly have to choose.

At the heart of the matter, Empathy is a choice - a choice that reflects what we value most inside and how we chose to exemplify that on the outside.

Will we go deeper than the surface with people? Or do we constantly live in a world where it's "me, myself, and I" all the time?

161

You know on your phone when you open up the camera and face it on yourself? The famous "selfie mode" kicks in, and all that matters is how you look, what and who is in the picture with you, and the main focus is primarily what you're doing. Though people may be in the picture as well, you only look at yourself. Well, empathy is deciding to flip the camera around. You still hold control over your life, but you become selfless enough to realize that there are things beyond us that matter more. People are hurting, people are rejoicing, and some are mourning. What a beautiful world it would be if we just took the time to say "I want to live a life that means something. Where my heart is in the right place so I can have empathy when I turn that camera."

Every single person has a story in this world. The beauty in this life is that everyone is different, yet we all seek similar things. We're more alike than we would take the time to realize. Empathy is sacred because it moves you to a place where we value others, which leads to building relationships and harvesting peace.

For a long time in my life, I prayed and asked God to bring change around me. I want people to have authentic love, meaningful relationships, and real faith. But then God brought me to 1 John 3:18 "let us love not with words or speech but rather actions and truth." This verse made me see that if I wanted change, I had to be the change. I need to be the change that GOD wants to see in the world. Not what I want to see or what I think is needed, but pray and ask for His kingdom to come and His will to be done. If my life is dedicated to being that change for the sole purpose of His glory rather than mine, then that is when the light is most magnified. Light was meant for dark place; change was meant to radiate this life that is so easily seen as dark.

Constantly I see change through empathy; and that is a defining feature in what builds your heart. Let us make the choice to reflect empathy by diving deeper than the surface with others. It is there we will find peace; residing in a river deep within the soul." -Jessica Jones

If only we all viewed the world the way this remarkable young soul perceives it. We all must decide to flip the camera off ourselves and become selfless enough to realize there are things beyond us that matter more. Empathy and compassion are the two gifts we give the world, and we become more and more alive each time we share that gift. To live beyond the surface reflects our deep rooted values of being called to serve and love - never stopping until we dive into the soul of each and every person we share the river with.

I needed to relearn how to treat people. Though I lost sight of it for many years, there has always been a part of me who has wanted to make everybody feel like a somebody. We all have our own story to tell, with pain I'm sure, but that doesn't mean we cannot be empathetic to what others are feeling and try our best to help them.

Even at my low point of running around clubs and partying my life away, I still remember making it a point to know every single employee down to the door security guard. It doesn't matter what your story is or what the other persons is, we should all do our best at putting ourselves in their shoes and walking their walk. Life is about perspective. Two people can view the same thing and find something entirely different that the other failed to see.

Dr. Wayne Dyer said, "If you change the way you look at things, the things you look at change." Rather than looking at the glass half full or half empty - shouldn't we acknowledge the fact that we're lucky enough to have a glass in the first place?

I needed to embrace new ways of thinking if I was ever going to find my peace. Just because I believed something to be true didn't mean someone else had to view it that way too. The moment I learned that other people are walking this Earth who have their own perspective and story to tell, the closer I came to finding Peace.

Being empathic is something most people fail to gain in their time here on this Earth. Yes, I needed to focus on myself for a while to better myself. I couldn't help others until I was in a place to be able to do so. But, I had finally reached that place because I now understood who should be in my life and who should not.

It is this reason why empathy was the hardest, and last, step in my Peace Quest. Most people are so concerned with their own walk and expressing their own views that they fail to learn how to be empathetic. Being empathetic is viewed as a weakness or 'pathetic' to most. I could not be one of these people if I wanted to find Peace in my life.

I believe Stephen R. Covey in, *The 7 Habits of Highly*

Effective People, said it best, "Seek first to understand, then to be understood." This was the key ingredient in me learning how to be empathetic. I had spent the last few months focusing on myself and what I needed to do to change. Now that I had done so, I needed to become aware of the needs of people around me and how to listen to those needs.

People Helpin' People (Continued)

I created a "People Helpin' People" list and wrote out 5-10 individuals I knew and ways in which I felt I could help them. It wasn't something extravagant or assertive, either. I simply wrote out a few people I knew and areas in their life or projects in which I could help them with. However big or small the task was, it didn't matter. I just began exploring ways of helping people but not pushing myself onto them and being quick to voice my opinion.

I made it one of my daily goals to find and help at least one person. I did this by seeking first to understand those needs, and then being understood. Sometimes, it was not every day, but just as long as I attempted it as much as I could, I was happy. Little things like helping someone move, developing a marketing plan, or talking them through a break-up. Whatever it was, I tried to find someone to help, and it made me feel the most fulfilled I'd felt in a long time.

The next thing I did was make a list of volunteer opportunities and how I could help. There were hundreds of them, monthly, right in the heart of San Diego. I learned that there was a strange device that gave me a layout of all these events…it was that little thing on my phone called *Google*. It literally took me five minutes to find something that best suited my capabilities and interests. I started feeding the homeless and teaching Autistic kids how to play baseball.

It changed my life. Volunteering once a month helped me appreciate the things I did have, and in the process, I got to help people who were not as fortunate as I was. This simple act alone softened my soul, bringing me ever closer to that long-awaited peace.

It's important to view the world as naturally good. The moment we start believing otherwise is when we find ourselves being one of the ones who makes it not. It was now time for me to go and be one of the ones who makes it good.

"The noblest art is that of making others happy."

– P.T. Barnum

Part Five - Empathy

1. You're not the only one here
    1. Understand that there are others on this Earth who may need our help
    2. Everyone we meet is fighting a battle in which we know absolutely nothing about. Seek first to understand, then to be understood.
    3. List five people you know in which you think you can help in some way or another.

2. Make it a daily goal to help someone
    1. Volunteer
    2. Help a friend move
    3. Simply listen to someone talk

If you'd like to begin your own Peace Quest, you can find the Ebook with worksheets and a detailed plan for Empathy on the website www. ThePeaceQuest.com

BUILDING A MASTER **P.E.A.C.E.**

"The best way to predict the future is to create it."

—Abraham Lincoln

Burn The Ships

As the story goes, in 1519 (yes, another history lesson), a Spanish captain and conquistador by the name of Hernando Cortez plotted to seize gold, silver, and precious jewels from the vast Aztec empire. He gathered 600 men with 11 ships and landed on the shores of the Yucatan in Mexico. These men – none of whom had sufficient armor or a burning desire to win – were infinitely outnumbered by an empire who had successfully conquered great generals and armies for over 600 years.

Cortez, realizing his men were already defeated in

their own minds, needed to find a way to ensure they were committed to victory. Rather than go the conventional route of giving an inspiring speech, he did something unusual that would alter the fate of the New World. Cortez gave the order to burn his own ships.

With his men questioning his reasoning and frightened for their lives, Cortez addressed them and said, "You see the boats going up in smoke. That means that we cannot leave these shores alive unless we win! We now have no choice—we win, or we perish!" The road to victory was clear for Cortez – Go All In, 100% committed. Remove the option of failure. No exit strategy to save their lives. No fall back plan. It was either win, or die.

Captain Hernando Cortez became the first man in 600 years to successfully conquer the Aztecs.

"Every person who wins in any undertaking must be willing to burn his ships and cut all sources of retreat. Only be doing so can one be sure of maintaining that state of mind known as a burning desire to win, essential to success."

-Napoleon Hill: *Think & Grow Rich*

What I Learned From Selling Popcorn At 10 Years Old.

I developed an entrepreneurial mind at a young age. When I was 10 years old, I started my first business.

Though my parents were relatively well off, they made me work for every dime they gave me. You know, the whole "Old Fashioned" thing… If I didn't work, I didn't get paid. It was as simple as that. So, I found ways of creating my own path early on in life.

I grew up in a town where there was a street dedicated to Christmas lights. Thousands of people would come nightly, from hundreds of miles away, just to stand in the freezing cold and stare at Christmas lights on Thoroughbred. Humans baffle me.

I knew the demand was there with literally thousands of people walking these lights. I thought to myself, what would I want if I was standing in the cold looking at Christmas lights? Then, one day, it clicked. They must be hungry, right?

I approached a buddy of mine, who fortunately lived on Thoroughbred, with the idea of renting a popcorn machine from Smart and Final and selling popcorn in front of his house. It was genius. We rounded up what little money we had, asked our parents to float what we couldn't cover, and then hit the ground running. We ran an extension cord from his house out to that popcorn machine and set up shop.

The very first night we made $700. I'm not kidding. I was stoked, and rich…for a 10-year-old. From then on, we sat out there every night and sold as much popcorn as people could eat. Soon enough, we were a one-stop shop. We had enough capital to pay off our parents for the start-up cash and began reinvesting it into the business. We sold everything from hot chocolate, candy, cider, nachos, and of course…our famous popcorn. It was my first business, and I made more money than I knew what to do with.

Word spread, and Thoroughbred quickly became saturated with coffee stands, caramel apples, and several hot chocolate & popcorn stands. I'm proud to say we were the first to do it and started quite the trend.

That was my first taste of understanding how to create my future out of thin air. The excitement and burning desire I felt from that first idea is a flame that still burns inside me today. Opportunity exists all around us, but as we get older, our vision becomes narrow and we fail to see the positive things this world has to offer. Over time, we let money and people affect our understanding of the way the world works. We give up hope on believing in ourselves and settle for what the world presents to us.

We lose our 'childish' creativity and begin to make decisions based on fear and impulse. We jump from job to job hoping we will have enough to pay rent next month. Survival mode takes over and all your passions go out the window. Soon enough, we become slaves to a job, confined to a system that brings us all to our knees by design. And we do it because it's what we think we have to do now, in order to do what we want to do later.

Money consumed my decision making for far too long. I couldn't do anything in my life without first asking myself the question, "How much is it and can I afford it?" Even questions regarding my career decisions. How am I going to afford advertising and marketing for my book? Will I be able to help people if I can't develop a steady income? Was writing the correct career move?

And those questions are almost always followed with a string of questions as to why I don't have the money I need to do whatever I want to do. And that almost always leads to me slipping back into the depression I've fought so hard to overcome.

Money consumes all of us. Why else would we work a job we hate, in a town we can barely afford, trying to impress people who don't even really care about us? All the while, we're becoming more and more depressed and doing whatever we can to avoid it all together.

Have you ever thought about what you would do with your time if money didn't exist? Would you still get up today and do what you are about to do?

Those are the types of questions you should be asking yourself. The questions that matter. The ones that make you think about the things you actually care about. Things like serving the world and chasing your passions over a paycheck.

So the million dollar question is, why on earth do we not Burn the Ships and go All-in on something we actually care about?

It's Time To Obsess Over The Right Things

I have an addictive personality. I know that, you know that, and everyone I've ever met probably knows that. If you look up "addictive personality" in the dictionary, I'd be willing to argue that my name is in there. But, I'm sure you have all gathered that by now.

I'm also well aware that my addictive personality will never go away. In fact, I've always appreciated my ability to obsess over things. Rather than sit here and claim I have control over it, I came up with an alternative.

I channel it into obsessing over the right things. For years I channeled it into partying, girlfriends, and Jack in the Box tacos (yum). But, not anymore. I made a list of things I actually care about, and want to accomplish, and now I channel all my energy into obsessing over those things. Now, I'm addicted to loving and being the best version of myself.

Jim Carrey, one of my favorite actors, said something in his commencement speech that will live with me forever:

> *"Fear is going to be a player in your life, but you get to decide how much. You can spend your whole life imagining ghosts, worrying about your pathway to the future, but all there will ever be is what's happening here, and the decisions we make in this moment, which are based in either love or fear.*
>
> *So many of us choose our path out of **fear disguised as practicality**. What we really want seems impossibly out of reach and ridiculous to expect, so we never dare to ask the universe for it...*

My father could have been a great comedian, but he didn't believe that was possible for him, and so he made a conservative choice. Instead, he got a safe job as an accountant, and when I was 12-years-old, he was let go from that safe job and our family had to do whatever we could to survive.

*I learned many great lessons from my father, not the least of which was that **you can fail at what you don't want, so you might as well take a chance on doing what you love**."*

I failed at doing all the things in which I didn't want and it resulted in my rock bottom. Once I decided to burn the ships, go all in and take a chance on doing something that I love - I have never felt more fulfilled and happy in all my life. If we are afraid to take the risk at living out our purpose and doing what we love, we will never know the heights in which we could have reached.

Our thoughts and beliefs shape what comes into our lives. The more negative we are, the more negativity we produce. The more positive thoughts we tell the Universe, the more positivity it produces for us. If we have the strength to ask the Universe for exactly what we want, it will give it to us. I am the proof because it gave it to me.

The Moment I've All But Waited For

As I stood, preparing to give a speech, in the backyard of my parents' home in Upland, California, I began to tear up. It was my 28th birthday - almost two years to the day since I had stood on the edge of my window deciding if I wanted to be alive anymore.

I looked around at the *community* of people who were gathered to not only celebrate my birthday, but my baptism too. That *community,* consisting of my new family, is the reason I'm here today. And they were there to witness my outward declaration of an inward transformation.

I thought about the past two years, how far I'd come and how my loving family had saved me from the lowest point of my life. In that moment, my sister and I met eyes and it was as if she looked right down into my soul and whispered, "You made it." I had never felt more renewed and happy in all my life.

There's a moment in your life when everything finally comes together. You realize what's important and what isn't. You learn to not only be kind to others, but kind to yourself too. You realize that things had to go wrong so you could learn how to appreciate them when they are right. You're happy to be alive and proud of the person you've fought so hard to become.

And then you smile. You smile because, you made it.

That moment, in which I had all but waited for, was here. The universe aligned and everything I asked of it finally came together. I had found my **P**urpose, **E**scaped my past, took **A**ction, **C**hanged my autopilot, and learned how to be **E**mpathetic to my surroundings. I was the happiest person in the world because I now understood the true meaning of life – to love and cherish every person we share the journey with.

I couldn't help but smile knowing that I was finally at peace.

It Only Takes One Moment...

I feel like this is the perfect moment to start rapping off Eminem's *Lose Yourself.* But, I'll spare you the cliché this time

You see, we all have this mentality that there will be sometime in the future when things are better. Let me tell you something in which you may not want to hear - you are where you are because that's where you have chosen to be. The best time to be who you want to be is right now. Your life can change in an instant. You hold all the power in your hands.

It only takes one moment to decide that you will no longer settle. One moment to separate yourself from the rest and go after what you want. One moment to no longer allow this world to decide what your future will hold. The only thing keeping you from your dream is yourself. Whatever you're feeling today is determining your future for you. You need to flip the script. Living a life full of regret is not living at all. You must decide if today is the day you will drastically change your life. No one can decide for you.

I know some of you are walking through the sh*t storm of your life. Faith is being able to stand in the middle of that storm and know you will plow your way through. When we're hurting and searching for peace and direction, people always tell us there will be light at the end of the tunnel. For me, I did not come to peace with my pain until I learned to shift my focus off the tunnel entirely.

Negative emotions are like quicksand. The more you struggle to get out of them the further into them you sink. Though there may be darkness clouding our lives and hope dwindling, the trick is finding ways to escape the darkness by doing positive things to change our lives. If we do not focus on the tunnel, we'll inevitably find the light. Bringing us to that long awaited Peace.

When you believe in yourself to go after what you want, there is no stronger force in the world. You won't know how it'll all work out in the beginning, I can promise you that. But, if you believe in yourself enough to Burn the Ships and go all-in - trust me when I tell you that it'll be worth the risk.

Success isn't built on what we do occasionally. It's built on what we do passionately. I now let my passions make my decisions for me. I am passionate about serving people, so I've made it my life's work to do so. If we are not doing what we are passionate about, and base our decisions off practicality, then we will never know what could've happened if we were willing to take the risk.

We can all be successful, it's just up to us to determine what our definition of success is. For a long time, my definition of success was skewed by the people I surrounded myself with. High rise condos, expensive cars, yachts, and tables at the best clubs were the things I found myself chasing. I learned to be all the things I did not want to be so I could understand how to be the person I was born to be. I mean, why is it that we fall? Isn't so we can learn how to pick ourselves up?

It took me 8 years to screw my life up, and 2 years to fix it. Now, I strive to be an honest man with a loving family one day whose vision is to impact as many lives as he can by teaching people to love who they are and use their past to better their future. If your desire is to be successful, then you better be selfless enough to flip the camera off yourself when the time comes.

It's now time for you to choose the next right thing. I mean, what's the purpose of living if we don't at least attempt at doing something extraordinary? Know that you can achieve greatness by trusting in yourself to chop wood and do what you were put on this earth to do. Believe in yourself and don't do it to prove everyone else wrong – do it to prove yourself right.

You don't need anyone to define what your happiness is. You know what it is in which you are supposed to do because you are unique in our own individual way. You were not put on this Earth by chance. It's time to ask the Universe for what you desire most and then trust it will give it to you. The path to success will not always be linear, but with persistence, belief in yourself, and a burning desire, you will attract the way.

I'll promise you this - It won't happen on the first night. And, it probably won't happen on the second night. But, after many nights of praying for a miracle, the day will come. You just have to believe it will.

One day, the universe will tap you on the shoulder and say, "You know what you dreamed it would be like? It's better than that." Three things make that happen - peace in your heart, purpose in your mind, and belief in yourself.

So, if today was the last day of your life, would you be at peace with your time spent here? If the answer is no, then it looks like you're ready for your own damn Peace Quest.

Time for you to build your own Master P.E.A.C.E. (see what I did there).

Final Words

Before I leave you, I want to ensure you are well equipped to go conquer the world. Let's recap!

10 Lessons From A Lost Twenty Something
(article taken from my blog - ryanwjones.com)

1. **Learn The Power Of "NO"**

   You really don't have to please everyone. Trying to impress people who care little about you, with money you don't have, along with drinking and partying, may result in an unbearable emptiness.

   You need to learn the Power of No. Once you do, it'll open up so much room for activities.

2. **Learn How to Weather the Sh*t Storm**

   Life is one giant sh*t storm. So, we need to understand that whatever road we're on, there will always be a storm coming and another obstacle we must overcome.

   And the only way to overcome these storms is by learning to fail forward and persevere… or as I like to call it, 'Weather the sh*t storm.'

3. **Find The Purpose And Passion That Drives You**

We all need purpose. Living without a sense of purpose is not living at all. Whatever your craft may be, we all have the urge to be useful in some way or another. Living as though we are making no difference in the world will only lead us to unhappiness. Understanding what your purpose is and why you are here will bring a fulfilling clarity to your life.

4. **Commit To Your Own Definition Of Success**

You need to understand success can and will be achieved by trusting in yourself to do exactly what you were put on this earth to do.

There's a difference between wishing to be successful and knowing. Those who wish for success, do not truly believe they are capable of achieving it. Those who know, commit to their own definition of success and are relentless in attaining it.

The true-life test is defining your own meaning of success, and walking the narrow path you've paved for yourself to get there.

5. **Stay in Your Own Lane**

   Stop worrying about what everyone else is doing because, in reality, no one actually knows what the hell they're doing. If you rely on other people for your own happiness it will result in your own misery.

   We can only be responsible for our own path. We need to let others have theirs.

6. **Change Your Autopilot**

   Have you heard my airplane joke? Never mind — it's over your head.

   If you want to drastically change your life, you must make drastic changes in your life. That means drastically changing your habits, developing a road map to success, and sticking to a regimented schedule.

   Don't Conform. Transform.

7. **Learn How to Chop Wood**

   No, I'm not talking about going in your backyard and hacking down a tree, Farmer John.

What I mean is wake up every single day with an ax, ready to go to work.

Dwayne "The Rock" Johnson said it best, "Success isn't overnight. It's when every day you get a little better than the day before. It all adds up."

8. **Exercise. And For You – Not For Everyone Else**
Exercising 3-5 times a week will give you a sense of accomplishment every day, skyrocketing your self-esteem. But, if you do it seeking the approval of others, you will end up quitting.

So, just do it for you. Do it because it makes you feel good. And because it makes getting four tacos at Jack in the Box way more acceptable

9. **"People Helpin' People" is a real thing**
Everyone we meet is fighting a battle in which we know absolutely nothing about. Make it a daily goal to help at least one person and it will change your life.

It's important to view the world as naturally good. The moment we start believing otherwise is when we find ourselves being one of the ones who makes it not.

10. In case you forgot, your parents are people too

You mean to tell me that my parents are humans? What a concept.

The moment you realize that every parent on this planet makes mistakes (including you when the time comes) and that maybe they are just trying to survive like you, everything changes.

You realize that maybe you were, indeed, an asshole. And that maybe they were just trying to help you not be an asshole.

So, call your mom, hug your pops – and tell them sorry...for being an asshole.

Okay, What Did You Learn About Yourself?

What is your Purpose and Mission Statement?

What are you 100% committed to?

What is your regimented schedule and daily routine? (Morning, Daytime, Evening)

What methods will you take to ensure you do not go back to your old ways?

How are you serving this world?

What is your definition of success?

What is your plan to obtain it?

** If you'd like to begin your own Peace Quest, you can find the Ebook with worksheets and a detailed plan on the website www.ThePeaceQuest.com

ACKNOWLEDGMENTS

Mom & Dad

You have shaped who I am today. I am forever grateful that you found it in your heart to accept my past and allowed me to grow into the person you always wanted me to be. You have taught me how to love, how to dream, and how living a life of character and dignity brings peace to your surroundings. I strive to be more like you with every new day. I can only hope that I am able to one day give my family the joy you have brought to my life. Not only are you the parents who pulled their child out of the worst place he has ever been - you're also the two best friends that have never left my side through it all. I love you more than words and I thank you from the bottom of my heart for always believing in me.

Austin

Though I was not always the brother I should have been, I want you to know that I now strive to be a person in your life you can always look up to. Thank you for standing by me and always encouraging me to be the older brother I know I can be. I love you and will always be in your corner rooting you on to be the best you can be. You amaze me more and more every day and I know you will conquer the world in whatever direction you decide. I'm very proud to be your brother.

Jessica

God blessed me with my own personal angel, and you are her. You are remarkable, in every way a person can be, and you inspire me to be the change in this world with every new day. You remind me constantly that we are called to be a light in this dark world. I am forever grateful that you saved my life and helped me find that light. Your soul radiates purity and selflessness, and we should all strive to be more like you. You will be the change in this world, and I am blessed to be able to walk along side and watch you do it. I love you more than you will ever know.

Mrs. Hunter

How does one address the person who made all of this possible? Maybe I should begin by ensuring there are no grammatical errors in this acknowledgment ;) You are the person who taught me how to write, and there would be no book without you. You inspire young minds with every passing day, and make it your mission to bring joy and laughter to each of your students. I am forever grateful for your willingness to edit this book - but more importantly, the time you continuously take in encouraging me to pursue my dreams. Thank you, Mrs. Hunter, for all that you do.

Mama B.

My Person. There are people who come in your life at various times, for various reasons. Some good, some bad. Some for a short time, some for a long time. And then, theres the people who come in your life and are there to stay. The ones you can count on to stay up until all hours of the night listening to you explain how you're going to change the world. The ones who will never stop believing in you, even when you no longer believe in yourself. B, you are this person for me and if it wasn't for you, I'd still be lost trying to navigate my way through the storm. Thank you, for not only editing the book, but for being my person through it all.

Aunty Jo

Though I love all my relatives dearly, you are at the top of the list (shhhh, don't tell anyone). I came to you at a time when I didn't know who else to turn to. You didn't hesitate to help me and have always been there regardless of the circumstance. You define unconditional love, and have never missed an opportunity to demonstrate that love to me wherever you could. I love you and want to thank you from the bottom of my heart for all that you have done for me. I am eternally grateful.

Kevin Jiminez

Confucius say man who do shitty things most of life one day realize it time to clean self up. You're the King of Confucius jokes, and I want to thank you for always being the guy to make me laugh even in my darkest of times. You called every day just to check in and see how I was doing when I was struggling. You have taught me what it means to be loyal. You encourage me to grow, while also pulling me back down to earth when I dream too big. You've taught me how to think logically and realistically about the things I want to accomplish. You will forever be my brother. Love you, Kevo.

God's Group of 1%er's

My dudes! This group alone is the true definition of community. We have created something truly special, and you guys have restored my faith. You all challenge me to grow in my relationship with Christ, while also encouraging me to pursue my dreams. Though I may have a background in pain, you all give me the hope that I will have a future in peace. Thank you for being a true testament to iron sharpens iron. Much love, dudes!

Brad Gardner

We've come a long way from that first donut. You have taught me many things on this journey - and there wasn't a time in my life where you didn't encourage me to be all that I could be. I hope you know how much I appreciate the things you have done for me in my time here. I can only hope that one day my son will challenge your son the way you have challenged me - always pushing me to be a better person then I was the day before. Thank you, maaaaan, for standing by me through it all.

Matt Wagner

The Wag Factor. You were my business partner, roommate, go-to wide receiver... and now, after everything we've gone through, I'm lucky enough to call you one of my lifelong friends. You accepted my apology, almost immediately, even when you shouldn't have. You didn't turn your back, and you helped me grow into the person I am today. I want to thank you for all that you have done and know that I will always be in your corner. Much love brotha.

Alan & Kenny

Yes, I lumped you two together because you're family, and you're forced to be okay with it because we're blood. Anyway, the two of you equally helped me more than I'm sure you will ever know. I came to you guys at my lowest points, all throughout my life, and you both did whatever you could to help me. You're the true definition of what it means to be family. Though I am thankful for the empathy you've shown me over the years, that does not mean I will go easy on you at Christmas when we pull out the Nerf guns and go to war. Some things I will just never be able to change about myself. May the odds be ever in my favor.

Chuck "Dad" Pender

I'm sorry, Dad ;-). You moved in at my worst, and there isn't a day that goes by where I'm not thankful for all the things you did for me in that time. Without even knowing you were doing so, you showed me more compassion than most would have moving into a situation like that. You taught me about that little thing called adulting (I think that's what the kids call it) and how to depend on yourself to get things done. Thank you for pushing me to be better and teaching me how to let go of things that don't better my life. I look forward to seeing what you accomplish in this life - witnessing first hand that you can accomplish anything you set your mind to. Make it a good day today, Chuckie. Much love, my dude.

Nicole Freeman

Neibs!!! You are just a different breed of human all together. You understand, all the way down to your core, how we should treat people on this Earth. You're independent yet completely selfless, and always look for the good in people. When I set out on this journey, I was unsure if I could even write. You were one of the first I showed it to, and you encouraged me to keep going even when I told myself not to. If it wasn't for you, there would be no book and I would still be searching for my purpose. Thank you for believing in me even when I didn't. I love you more than words and am so blessed to call you one of my closest friends.

Travis Blair, Taylor Pattronette, Zac Fullmer

I can't think of a time when the three of you were not in my corner. Even when I was running around being mister club guy and treating people terribly - you guys still reached out to see how I was doing and to make sure I wasn't getting too carried away with partying. You guys always called to check in on my Mom and make sure she was feeling better - and were all there for me when I went through my dark time. You were waiting on the other side with open arms and were ready to pick up right where we had left off. I want to thank you for being the people I could always count on. Much love, dudes. - Assclown

Tony Robbins & Joe Duncan

Can we be friends? Even if it's only for like a day or two. I know it's all kinds of creepy that I try so hard to be like you - but, if you're going to dream, you might as well dream big, right? Anyway, thank you both for being the type of people we should all strive to be like. I know you both have helped countless people achieve their goals of finding success and I'm just another to add to the list - but, I want you both to know how thankful I am that I stumbled across your words. If it wasn't for you, I have no idea where I would be. The two of you took part in saving my life, and I am forever indebted to you. I hope that one day I am lucky enough to meet you both (then maybe it wont be so creepy).

That's all I got for now - stay tuned, friends ;)

#Lost20Something

ABOUT THE AUTHOR

I feel like Wikipedia should have a normal person division... "Ryan Jones is an American Regular Human. He hasn't done a whole lot yet, but tries really hard and we respect that. Keep on keepin' on, Ryan."

But, if we must, here is a taste of my journey...

I have a background in pain.

If you're here reading this, however, I have some good news for you... we all must feel some sort of pain in our lives before we experience a breakthrough into finding peace and purpose for being here.

I am no different. I was lost in a dark storm and I allowed that darkness to cloud my life for many years. For a long time, I was breathing, but not yet alive. I didn't start living until I no longer allowed that darkness to hinder me from becoming the person I always dreamed of becoming. Sometimes, to find who we are we must lose who we were.

I believe that inner peace is the new success in the world we live in today.

So, I created a Five-Step process to finding P.E.A.C.E in your life (Purpose, Escaping your past, Action, Change, and Empathy) in hopes of guiding as many people I can to living a successful, happy, and purpose-filled life.

My great hope is that our mission on this quest of life will not be to simply survive but to come alive through passion, purpose and ultimately peace. I believe that we become what we are committed to. I may have a background in pain, but I am committed to a future in P.E.A.C.E.

Facebook - @ryanwjones99
Instagram - @ryanwilljones
Twitter - @ryanwilljones
Website - ryanwjones.com

Printed in the United States
By Bookmasters